BREAS

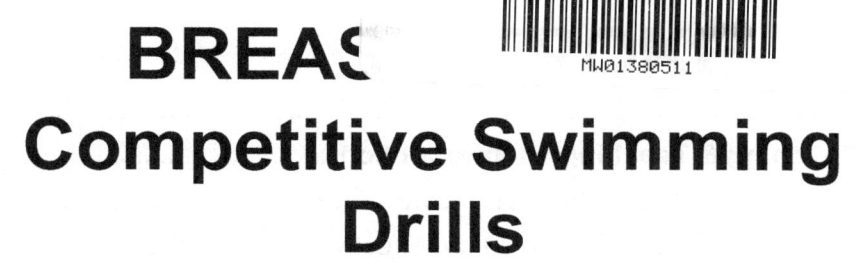

MW01380511

Competitive Swimming Drills

**Over 60 BREASTSTROKE Drills Improve Technique |
Add Variety|
For Coaches | For Teachers | For Swimmers**

First edition published in the United Kingdom in 2020
Copyright © Eatsleepswimcoach

https://eatsleepswimcoach.com

Contents

Welcome

A very warm welcome to **'Breaststroke Competitive Swimming Drills'.**

About this publication

This publication provides coaches, teachers and swimmers with a series of tried and tested competitive breaststroke swimming drills.
- These drills can be used to develop and maintain a particular, or range of breaststroke skill/s.
- They can be easily incorporated and adapted into your training or teaching programme, whether you coach or teach rookie or national swimmers.

Delivering the technical demands of our sport

Competitive swimming can be a gruelling sport, requiring swimmers to undertake many hours of repetitive training each week, in pursuit of excellence.
- Developing a training or teaching programme that delivers the technical demands of our sport, while at the same time adding variety to your sessions can be an ongoing process.
- This can be both difficult and time-consuming to achieve.
- Training or teaching programmes without fresh stimuli are in real danger of demotivating swimmers, coaches and teachers alike.
- Over the past twenty-five plus years as a head coach, coach and teacher, I have managed to collate a large portfolio of competitive breaststroke drills.
- I have used these to develop many young competitive

breaststroke swimmers from club to county, regional/state and national levels, the best of which are published here.

Publication focus

This publication focuses on the stroke's key technical areas.
● Each has its own dedicated chapter, breaking down the stroke into its key constituent parts, to help both the coach, the teacher and the swimmer develop and maintain a great breaststroke.

About Us - EatSleepSwimCoach

EatSleepSwimCoach is a competitive swimming website.
● Our team includes swimmers, swimming parents, teachers and coaches.
● With over 50 years of combined competitive swimming experience, both in the pool and open water.
● We provide swimming advice, drills, exercises, hacks, insight and tips.
● We produce publications, posts, articles and digital downloads on a wide range of swimming subjects.
● These include stroke technique, training drills and how to optimise training and competitive performance.
For further information please visit our website by using the following link: https://eatsleepswimcoach.com/

Facebook Group

EatSleepSwimCoach administers the **Competitive Swimming Exchange** Facebook Group.
● This is a competitive swimming group to help exchange ideas and information to collectively improve the sport we love.
● It's an international group for all swimmers, coaches, teachers, masters, triathletes and swimming parents.
● In fact, it's for all those who are interested in competitive swimming, either in the pool or in open water.
For further information about joining this group please use the following   link:
https://www.facebook.com/groups/thecompetitiveswimmingexchange

Coaching & Teaching an Introduction

Competitive swimming training

Competitive swimming training requires the swimmer to perform repetitive technical and physical drills, to master a set of key skills.
• This enables them to perform to the best of their ability, when under the pressure of competition.
• Repetitive training enables the swimmer to adapt their training to their 'muscle memory'*, enabling them to automatically perform as taught during competition.
(*muscle memory - the ability to reproduce a movement without conscious thought, acquired as a result of frequent repetition of that movement)

• If the training is repetitively performed with a perfect technique, then the muscle memory will store this perfect technique.
• However, if the training is repetitively performed with a poor technique, then the muscle memory will store this poor technique.
• Once a poor technique has been stored, this can be very difficult to correct.
• For any coach or teacher, it is important that they 'consistently and persistently' incorporate perfectly performed drills into their training or teaching programmes to reinforce and develop a great butterfly technique.

Swimming drills

I introduce drills into every training session.
• I incorporate them into every warm-up routine.

- I also conduct a twenty-minute 'drills based' activity after the warm-up, before the swimmers become fatigued.
- I have found this is long enough to teach drills correctly and short enough for swimmers to maintain focus.

Make progress slowly

I have found that it pays to be patient when introducing a new drill.
- Some swimmers quickly learn some techniques and struggle to learn others.
- Coaches and teachers should use multiple coaching and teaching formats.
- Some swimmers may prefer to learn via verbal or written communication.
- Other swimmers may prefer to learn via a physical demonstration.
- Wherever possible, I use swimmers who have mastered a technique to demonstrate specific drills.
- I have found that using a senior swimmer to demonstrate drills to junior swimmers, is a very effective way of getting my coaching points across.

I have found the use of fins very useful while introducing some of these drills to younger or less experienced swimmers.
- It can help them to increase their speed and power and can also help to increase the swimmer's confidence and help reduce the chance of them becoming fatigued.

Only once a good technique has been mastered should the level of difficulty be gradually increased.
- These drills can be adapted and developed accordingly, by increasing the distance, intensity or decreasing the target time.

Training aids

Resistance, assistance and variety can also be added by the introduction of training aids such as:
- Bungee cords
- Drag belts/shorts
- Hand paddles
- Kickboards
- Pull buoys
- Snorkels
- Swim fins

Safety First

• Always ensure the safety of the swimmers in your charge, whilst carrying out any drill.

• Whether starting in the water or from a dive, please ensure your swimmers have enough room to allow the correct and unhurried execution of the drill.

• When starting any drill that requires a dive, please ensure the swimmer can perform a racing dive safely and they have achieved the relevant competitive start accreditation.

Please note the drills contained in this publication are performed in a 25m pool.

• Please make the relevant adjustments if you coach or teach in a pool of a different distance.

I hope you find this publication useful, enjoy your coaching and teaching.

Coach Arthur

Chapter 1: Breaststroke an Introduction

Breaststroke is the slowest and least efficient of all the competitive strokes.

● Although breaststroke can generate effective propulsion from both the arms stroke and the leg kick, the recovery of both the arms and the legs, creates large amounts of drag, slowing the stroke dramatically.

● Swimmers have to work hard to make the stroke effective.

● As a result, competitive breaststroke requires a high degree of power, strength, endurance, speed, and coordination to generate the required speed for each stroke.

● Being the slowest competitive stroke, breaststroke is usually the decisive leg of most individual medleys.

The key technical components of a great breaststroke

● Ability to 'catch' (feel) the water, assisted by sculling and stroke counting drills.

● A strong, quick and powerful arm pull.

● A powerful lunge into a kick.

● A strong and effective leg kick.

● An effective glide phase aided by a great streamlining technique.

● The stroke timing ensuring that the three phases of the stroke, the pull, the kick and the glide combine for an efficient stroke.

● Efficient starts, turns & finishes.

● Which are aided by an effective underwater leg kick and tight streamlining.

The timing sequence for a great breaststroke

To achieve a fast and effective breaststroke, swimmers must maintain a smooth balanced and coordinated stroke combined with the correct tempo.

● This should be maintained throughout the stroke's three distinct phases a strong, quick **pull**, a powerful leg **kick** and a streamlined **glide**.

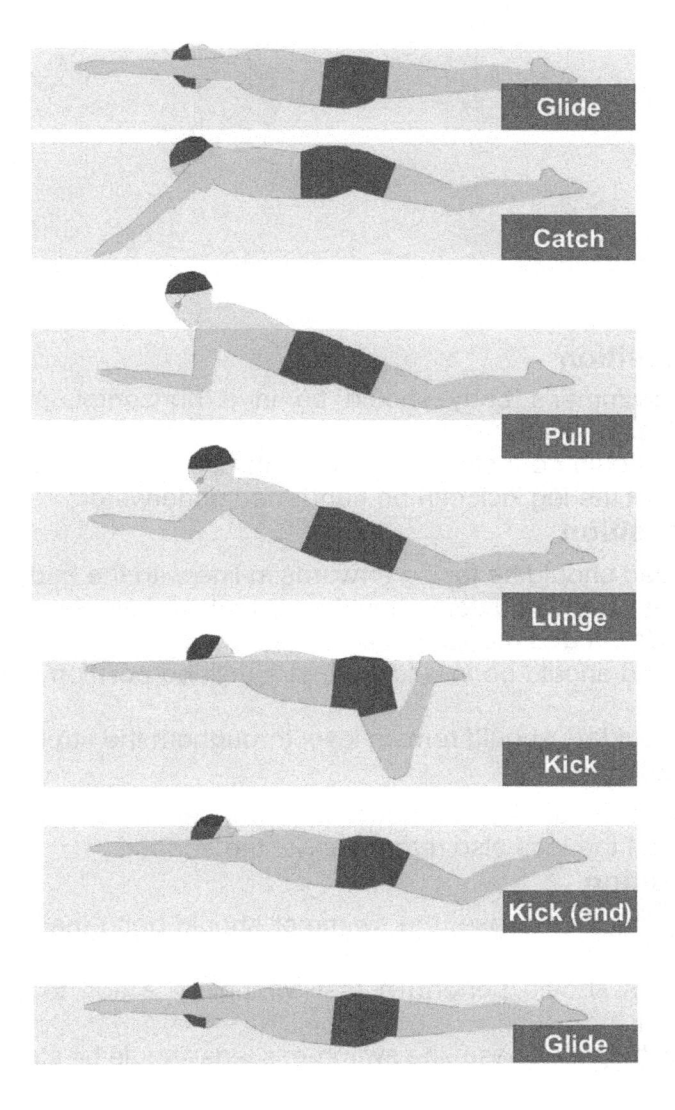

The drills contained in this guide will allow swimmers to progressively develop these key components and add them to their stroke.

1.1: The correct position for an effective breaststroke

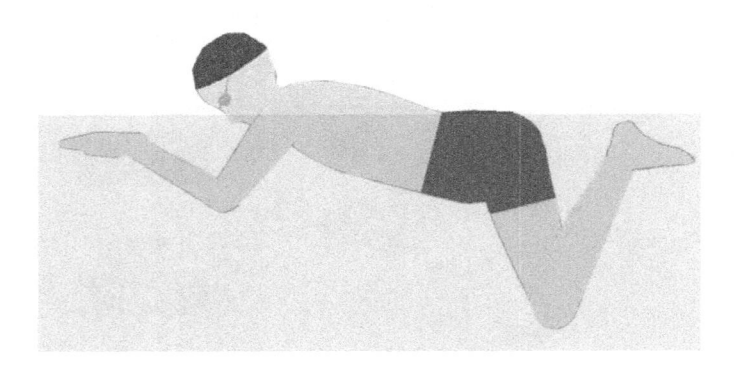

Body position
- The swimmer's body should be in a horizontal, prone and streamlined position.
- There should be a slight slope from the swimmer's head to their feet so that the leg kick can be performed underwater.

Head position
- The head should be facing forwards in line with the body.
- The neck and shoulders should be as relaxed as possible to aid the arm action and reduce strain.
- The head should be in a tucked, streamlined position during the glide.
- The shoulders should remain level throughout the stroke.

Hips position
- The hips should be just under the surface of the water to help ensure that the legs also remain under the surface.

Leg position
- During the kick phase, the swimmer should bend their knees to facilitate their heels being brought up towards their buttocks.
- The legs should perform a fast 'whipping' action to drive the propulsion.
- During the glide phase, the swimmer's legs should be streamlined

and under the surface of the water.

Feet position

● During the kick phase, the swimmer should turn their feet out to provide a large surface area to aid propulsion.

● They should then push their heels and feet backwards and outwards, in a fast simultaneous and continuous leg action.

● The feet should be in a pointed (plantar flexion) position during the glide phase, which helps to reduce drag.

Chapter 2: The Leg Kick

Introduction: The major propulsive force in breaststroke is derived from the leg kick.
● Therefore, it is important to regularly perform breaststroke leg drills within your training programme.
● Many swimmers find the breaststroke leg kick difficult to master and they may require extra care and attention.

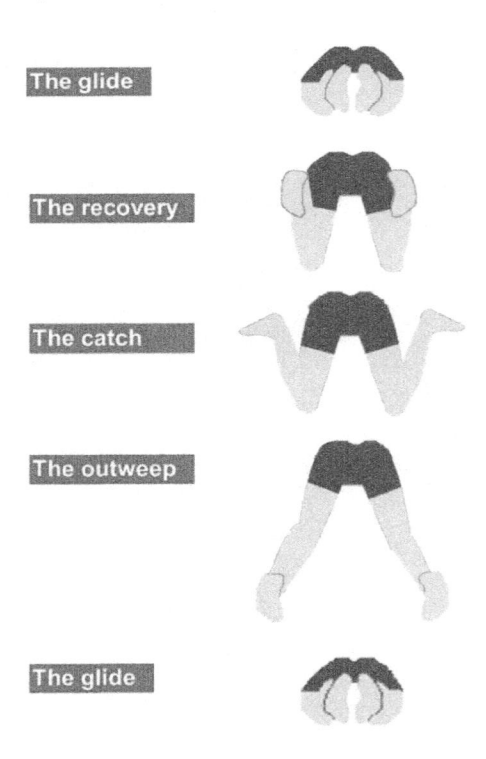

The glide

The recovery

The catch

The outweep

The glide

Key components of an effective breaststroke leg kick

The glide
- The swimmer should adopt a tight streamlined position.
- Their hands should be parallel, with their thumbs touching

The recovery
- As the swimmer completes the propulsive phase of their arm stroke (the insweep).
- They should bend their knees to facilitate their heels being brought up towards their buttocks, at speed.
- The swimmer should ensure that they bring their knees up towards their buttocks, to help ensure a full and powerful kick.
- They should ensure that their feet are in a pointed (plantar flexion) position

The catch
- As soon as the swimmer's heels are close to their buttocks, the swimmer should rotate their feet outwards, at an approximate ninety degrees angle, providing a large surface area to provide propulsion.

Outsweep
- As soon as the swimmer has completed their catch.
- They should then push their heels and feet backwards and outwards, in a fast simultaneous and continuous leg action.

The glide
- The leg kick should be performed with a circular motion, finishing in a streamlined position, ready to begin the next stroke cycle.

2.1: 'Teddy bear' kicking

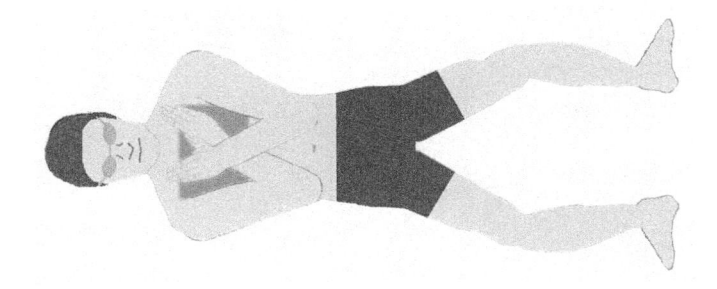

Purpose: This is an introductory drill to help develop the swimmer's breaststroke kicking technique.

How to perform this drill: The swimmer should start this drill from a push and glide from the wall at the end of the pool, in a supine position (on their back).

● They should hold a kickboard across their chest as if they are cuddling a 'teddy bear' and while performing a series of breaststroke leg kicks.

● They should bring their knees up to their full extent while starting the leg kick action.

● The swimmer should have their feet turned outwards during the catch phase.

● They should complete the leg kick action in a streamlined position.

● The swimmer should ensure that their knees are below the surface whilst kicking.

● They should repeat this drill for one length/lap of the pool (25m).

Coaching Points: The swimmer should ensure that at the end of the kicking action, the swimmers heals are together in a tight streamlined (planta flex) position, to ensure that the drag is reduced, and maximum propulsion is achieved.

2.2: Heals to hands supine

Purpose: This drill further helps to develop the swimmer's breaststroke kicking technique.

How to perform this drill: The swimmer should start this drill from a push and glide from the wall at the end of the pool, in a supine

position (on their back), with their arms by their sides.
- The swimmer should bring their knees up to their full extent while starting the leg kicking action.
- They should ensure that their heals touch their hands, whilst doing so.
- The swimmer should have their feet turned outwards during the catch phase.
- They should complete the leg kick action in a tight streamlined position.
- The swimmer should ensure that their knees are below the surface whilst kicking.
- They should repeat this drill for one length/lap of the pool (25m).

2.3: Supine streamlined kicking

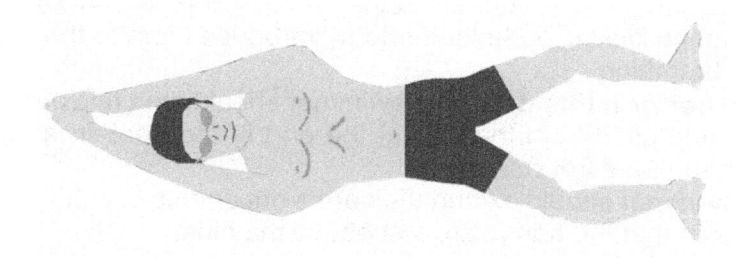

Purpose: This drill further helps to develop the swimmer's breaststroke kicking technique.

How to perform this drill: The swimmer should start this drill from a push and glide from the wall at the end of the pool, in a supine position (on their back), with their arms fully extended in a streamlined position.
- They should then proceed with a powerful leg kicking action.
- The swimmer should have their feet turned outwards during the catch phase.
- They complete the leg kick action in a tight streamlined position.
- The swimmer should ensure that their knees are below the surface whilst kicking.
- They should repeat this drill for one length/lap of the pool (25m).

2.4: Heels to hands prone

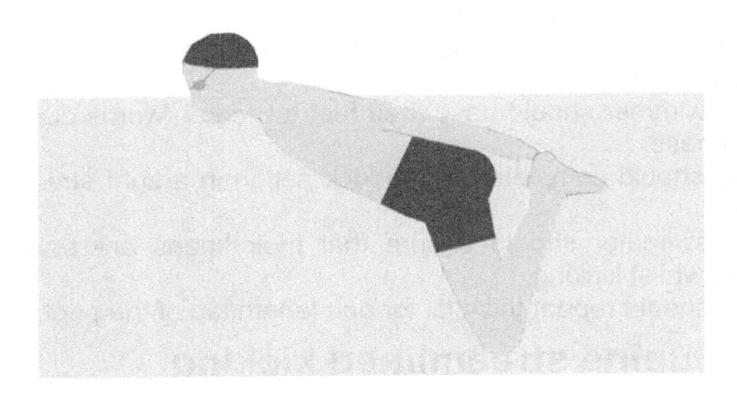

Purpose: This drill further helps to develop the swimmer's breaststroke kicking technique and to introduce them to the timing of their breathing.

How to perform this drill: The swimmer should start this drill from a push and glide from the wall at the end of the pool, in a prone position (on their front).

• The swimmer should extend their arms out and up in a 45-degree position so that the hands are just above the hips.

• At the start of the leg kick action the swimmer should bring their heels up to touch their hands.

• The major difference in performing this drill on their front is that it introduces the swimmer to the breathing and timing of the stroke.

• As the swimmer kicks back strongly, the swimmer can take a breath as the leg propulsion drives them forward.

• They should ensure that they breathe to the front and have their chin on the surface while doing so.

• The swimmer should repeat this drill for one length/lap of the pool (25m).

2.5: Prone streamlined kicking

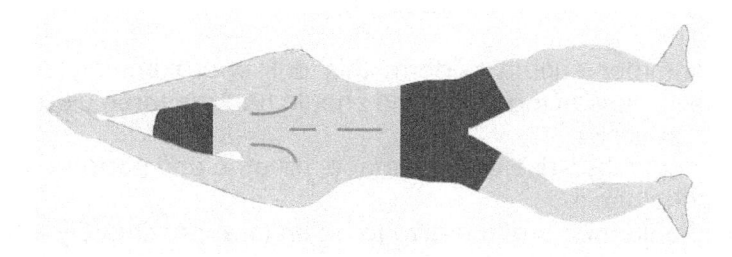

Purpose: This drill further helps to develop the swimmer's breaststroke kicking technique and to introduce the swimmer to the timing of their breathing.

How to perform this drill: The swimmer should start this drill from a push and glide from the wall at the end of the pool, in a prone position (on their front) streamlined position, with their arms fully extended.

● This drill should be performed just below the surface of the water.

● They should then proceed with a powerful breaststroke leg kicking action, rising to the surface to breathe.

● The swimmer should ensure that they time their breathing just after the glide phase and at the beginning of the catch phase.

● They should ensure that they breathe to the front and have their chin on the surface while doing so.

● The swimmer should repeat this drill for one length/lap of the pool (25m).

2.6: 3 kicks underwater, 1 full stroke

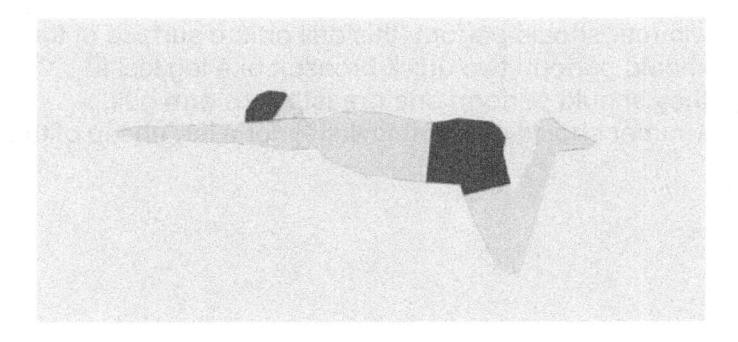

Purpose: This drill further helps to develop a powerful breaststroke leg kick.

How to perform this drill: The swimmer should start this drill from a push and glide from the wall at the end of the pool, in a prone position (on their front) streamlined position, with their arms fully extended.

- The swimmer should perform this drill approximately a metre under the surface of the water and should perform three underwater breaststroke kicks.
- They should then rise to the surface, breathe and perform one full breaststroke stroke.
- They should then surface dive to again to approximately a metre under the surface of the water and repeat the drill.
- The swimmer should repeat this drill for one length/lap of the pool (25m).

2.7: 2 kicks 1 pull

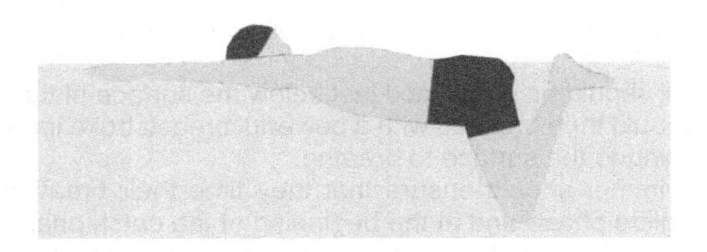

Purpose: This drill helps to further develop a powerful breaststroke leg kick.

How to perform this drill: The swimmer should start this drill from a push and glide from the wall at the end of the pool, in a prone position (on their front) streamlined position, with their arms fully extended.

- The swimmer should perform this drill on the surface of the water
- They should perform two quick breaststroke leg kicks.
- Then they should perform one breaststroke arm pull.
- The swimmer should repeat this drill for one length/lap of the pool (25m).

2.8: Kicking with a kickboard

Purpose: This drill helps to further develop the breaststroke leg kick.

● The use of a kickboard is an excellent way of developing an effective leg kick by isolating the swimmer's legs.

How to perform this drill: The swimmer should start this drill from a push and glide from the wall at the end of the pool, in a prone position (on their front) while holding a kickboard, while keeping their head out of the water.

● The swimmer should ensure that their arms are extended fully.

● They should hold the kickboard at the top edge and rest their forearms on the kickboard.

● The swimmer should then perform a controlled and powerful breaststroke leg kick.

● They should ensure that they finish the kick correctly with their feet in a pointed (plantar flexion) position.

● The swimmer should repeat this drill for one length/lap of the pool (25m).

2.9: Resistance kicking with a kickboard

Purpose: This is an excellent drill for further developing and maintaining a strong breaststroke leg kick by adding additional resistance.

How to perform this drill: The swimmer should start this drill from a push and glide from the wall at the end of the pool, in a prone position (on their front) while holding a kickboard, while keeping their head out of the water.

• The swimmer should perform a controlled and powerful breaststroke leg kick.

• The swimmer should hold the kickboard vertically upright so that half of the kickboard is under the surface.

• For increased resistance, the swimmer can hold the kickboard horizontally upright, so again half of the kickboard is under the surface.

• The swimmer should repeat this drill for one length/lap of the pool (25m).

2.10: Kicking builds

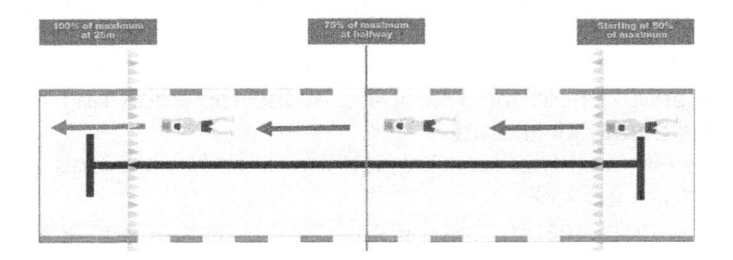

Purpose: An introductory drill to speed play which helps develop speed and power into the breaststroke leg kick.

How to perform this drill: The swimmer should start this drill from a push and glide from the wall at the end of the pool, in a prone position (on their front) while holding a kickboard, while keeping their head out of the water.

• The swimmer should start kicking at 50% of their maximum kicking speed and should gradually increase the speed of their kick over one length.

• The swimmer should be around 75% of their maximum kicking speed at half-way and be close to reaching their maximum kicking speed as they approach the finish of the length/lap.

• This drill should be performed over short distances, in sets of single lengths/laps, with a 20 to 30-second rest interval between each length, as the emphasis of this drill should be a great kicking technique, as well as kicking speed.

2.11: Vertical breaststroke kicking

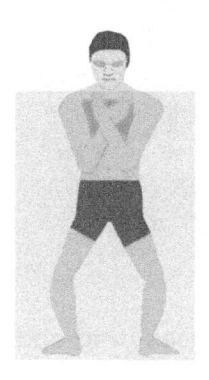

Purpose: Vertical breaststroke kicking is a great drill for developing a powerful breaststroke leg kick and improving ankle flexibility.

How to perform this drill: The swimmer should start this drill in water deep enough for them to vertically kick without touching the bottom of the pool.

● They should adopt a vertical body position in the water.
● They should perform a powerful and steady breaststroke leg kick.
● They should perform a slow sculling action with their hands.
● The swimmer should bob up and down as the result of each kick.
● Inexperienced or younger swimmers may wish to use a kickboard while learning this drill.

Coaching point: The swimmer should ensure that they do not raise their knees too high during this drill, as this could result in them lowering themselves in the water.

Variations: The swimmer can increase the intensity of the leg kick required, in four stages

● Level 1: By folding their arms across their chest.
● Level 2: By raising their shoulders out of the water.
● Level 3: By raising their hands and forearms out of the water.
● Level 4: By raising their arms out of the water, in a streamline position.

Chapter 3: Streamlining

Effective streamlining reduces drag and maintains the swimmer's speed.

● Therefore, streamlining can increase the distance achieved by the swimmer during the starts, turns and transitions*.

*transitions the phase from a start or a turn, where the swimmer breaks out into a full stroke.

● The ability to perform an effective streamlined position is a key swimming skill and should be regularly developed, practised and maintained, especially for younger developing swimmers.

How to perform an effective streamline position

To perform an effective streamline position, the swimmer should be in a long torpedo shape, where the fingers, hands, arms, head, body, legs and feet are on the same level plane.

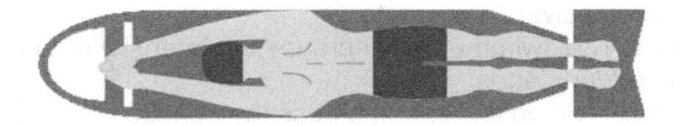

Fingers

The swimmer's fingers should be closed and pointing in the direction they wish to travel.

Hands

Their hands should be placed on top of one another, with the thumb of the upper hand wrapped around the outside of the lower hand,

locking them into position.
● They should be pointing in the direction they wish to travel.

Arms

The swimmer's arms should be fully extended to narrow the shoulders.
● They should be pointing in the direction they wish to travel.
● There should be no bend at the elbows.
● To facilitate this, the swimmer's biceps should be squeezed tightly at the rear of the swimmer's head and not pressing against their ears.

Head

Their head should be positioned so that the swimmer's biceps are squeezed tightly at the rear of the swimmer's head, to facilitate a straight streamlined arm position.

Coach Arthur says: "When the swimmers are squeezing their biceps against their head, they should do so behind their ears.
● Not only is the head a little narrower there, which results in better streamlining, but by doing so it narrows the shoulders, resulting in a more effective streamlined position.
● Some coaches prefer for their swimmers to place their chin on their chest and squeeze their arms behind their head.
● I recommend trying both positions to see which one you prefer".

Body

Their body should be in a flat and horizontal position with the swimmer's core engaged.

Engaging a swimmer's core

Engaging the core muscles ensures that they are correctly aligned, to help support and perform certain swimming drills and skills effectively.
● To engage their core, the swimmer should continue to breathe normally.
● They should then tighten/contract their stomach muscles while drawing their navel towards their spine.

Core strength development

To effectively engage their core whilst performing underwater

dolphin kicking, the swimmer should develop their core strength.
● They should perform core development training exercises such as crunches and planks as a regular part of their dryland/ land training programme.

Legs

The swimmer's legs should be straight and closed tightly together, with no bend at the knees.

Feet

Their feet should be in a pointed (plantar flexion) position, which reduces drag and places the feet in the optimum position for maximum propulsion.

3.1: Push & glide in the prone position

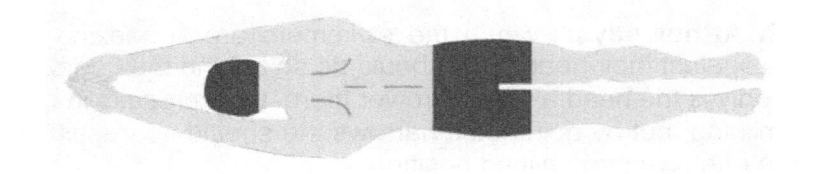

Purpose: This is a classic introductory streamlining drill.
How to perform this drill: The swimmer should start this drill from a push and glide from the wall at the end of the pool.
● They should focus on a very tight streamlining, about half a metre under the surface.
● They should attempt to get past the turn flags with their head (a good attempt) or their feet (a better attempt), before breaking out to the surface.
● They should ensure that they perform a strong push off the wall.
● The swimmer should ensure that they do not perform any kicking or body undulation movements.
● The coach should mark where the swimmer 'breaks out' to the surface on the poolside.

Coach Arthur says: To achieve an effective push off the pool wall, swimmers should ensure that their feet are firmly planted on the pool wall.
● Ideally shoulder-width apart and that their knees are bent at approximately ninety degrees.

3.2: Starfish drill

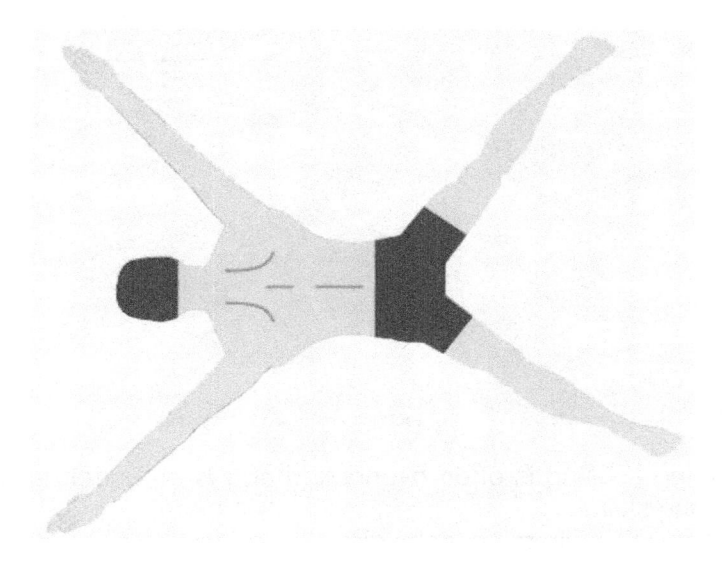

Purpose: This is an excellent drill for demonstrating the effectiveness of tight streamlining.

How to perform this drill: The swimmer should start this drill from a push and glide underwater in a streamlined prone position, about half a metre under the surface.

• As soon as the swimmer has left the wall, they should open both their arms and legs into a forty-five degrees position.

• This non-streamlined position should result in the swimmer almost coming to a complete stop in the water.

• This should demonstrate to the swimmer, the effectiveness of tight streamlining.

Chapter 4: Sculling

Swimming sculling is often overlooked and is an undervalued key swimming skill.
● Sculling is a swimming technique, which focuses on the pitch and position of the swimmer's hands and forearms in the water.
● This develops the swimmer's sense of the pressure in the water and increases their ability to **'feel the water'**.
● This enables them to gain **maximum purchase** of the water.
● Which in turn results in them obtaining increased **propulsion and lift** through the water.
● The correct hand shape, with fingers very slightly apart and hands slightly cupped.

To obtain the correct hand position for sculling
● The swimmer should place their hands on the cheeks of their face, ensuring that their fingers are very slightly apart.
● They should then remove their hands from their face, whilst keeping their fingers slightly apart.
● Their hands should now be in the optimum position for effective sculling.

4.1: Front-end scull

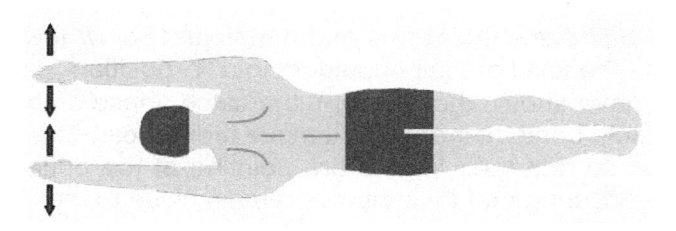

Purpose: This drill helps to develop the swimmer's out sweep at the front-end of the breaststroke stroke.

How to perform this scull: The swimmer should start this drill with a push and glide from the end of the pool, the swimmer should start to kick in a horizontal/prone position, whilst performing a slight flutter kick.

● They should place their arms and hands just below the surface, level with their shoulders.

● The swimmer should scull by moving their hands from side to side, with a thumbs up scull on the in sweep and with a thumbs down scull on the out sweep.

● They should repeat this drill for one length/lap of the pool (25m).

4.2: The catch scull

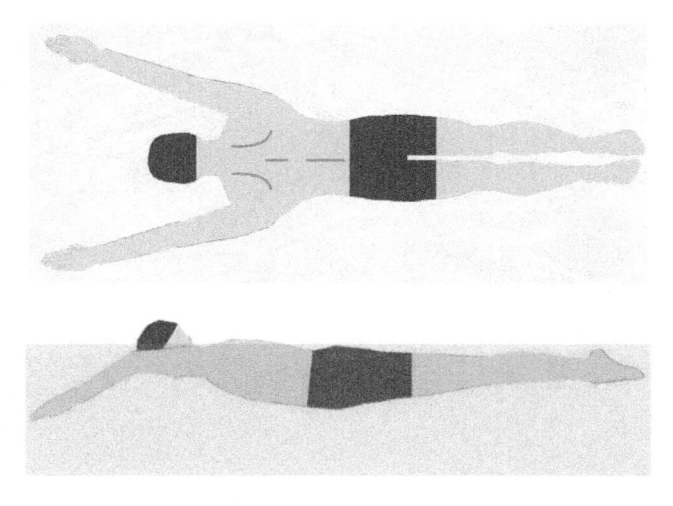

Purpose: This drill helps to develop a swimmer's catch.

How to perform this scull: The swimmer should start this drill with a push and glide from the end of the pool, the swimmer should start to kick in a horizontal/prone position, whilst performing a slight flutter kick.

- They should place their arms and hands just below the surface, just outside the level of their shoulders in a 'Y' position.
- The swimmer should then perform the catch phase of the pull.
- They should bend their arms and move their forearms and hands downwards so that their fingers are pointing at the bottom of the pool while ensuring that their elbows remain close to the surface.
- They should recover their arms underwater, back to the starting 'Y' position.
- The swimmer should repeat this drill for one length/lap of the pool (25m).

Variations: Once mastered the swimmers can perform three catch sculls, then one full breaststroke stroke.

- They can also perform this drill with a pull buoy.

Chapter 5: The Arm Stroke

Introduction: The arm pull in breaststroke is the secondary propulsive force.

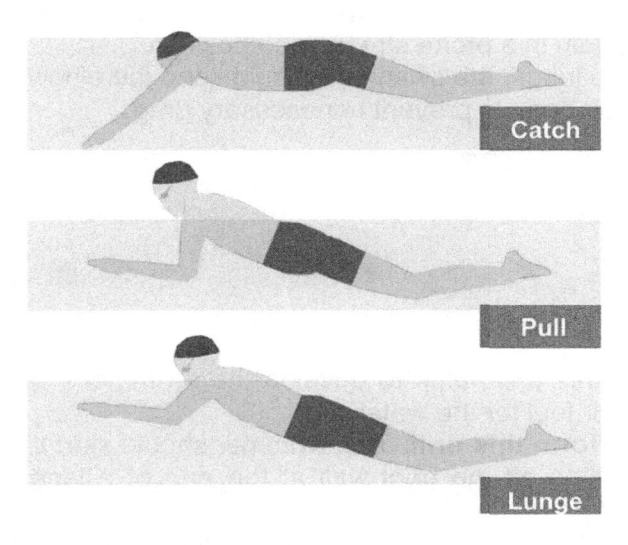

The key components of an effective breaststroke arm pull are

The out sweep

● The swimmer should scull with their palms turned slightly outwards, and with their arms moving level just under the surface until they are just outside the width of their shoulders.

The catch

- The catch is the start of the propulsive phase of the breaststroke arm pull
- At the end of the out sweep, the swimmer should bend their arms and moves their forearms and hands downwards, so that their fingers are pointing towards the bottom of the pool while ensuring that their elbows remain close to the surface.

The in sweep

- The in-sweep is the main propulsive phase of the arm stroke and should be the quickest part of the arm stroke.
- At the end of the catch the swimmers should move their arms backwards, inwards and upwards so that their hands are below their chest and they are pushing the water backwards.

The lunge

- At the end of the in-sweep, the swimmer should drive their arms and chest forward until their arms are fully extended again, and they are once again in a prone streamlined position.
- During the lunge, the swimmer should keep the elbows tucked in close to their body to prevent unnecessary drag.

5.1: I & Y arms

Purpose: This drill helps to develop the swimmer's breaststroke pull and their feel for the water.

How to perform this drill: The swimmer should start this drill with a push & glide off the pool wall at the end of a lane, in a tight streamlined prone (on their front) position.

- They should break out to the surface, while still holding the tight streamlined position. (The I position)
- The swimmer should start to perform a steady freestyle flutter kick.
- They should then perform an outward (front-end) sculling action into the Y position.
- Then they should then perform an inwards (front-end) sculling back into the I position.
- *For further information, see Chapter 4 Sculling: Front-end scull.*

- Once back into the I position the swimmer should perform a full breaststroke stroke, where they can take a breath.
- The swimmer should repeat this drill for one length/lap of the pool (25m).
- Once mastered, the swimmer may perform this drill using hand paddles.

5.2: Catch-up

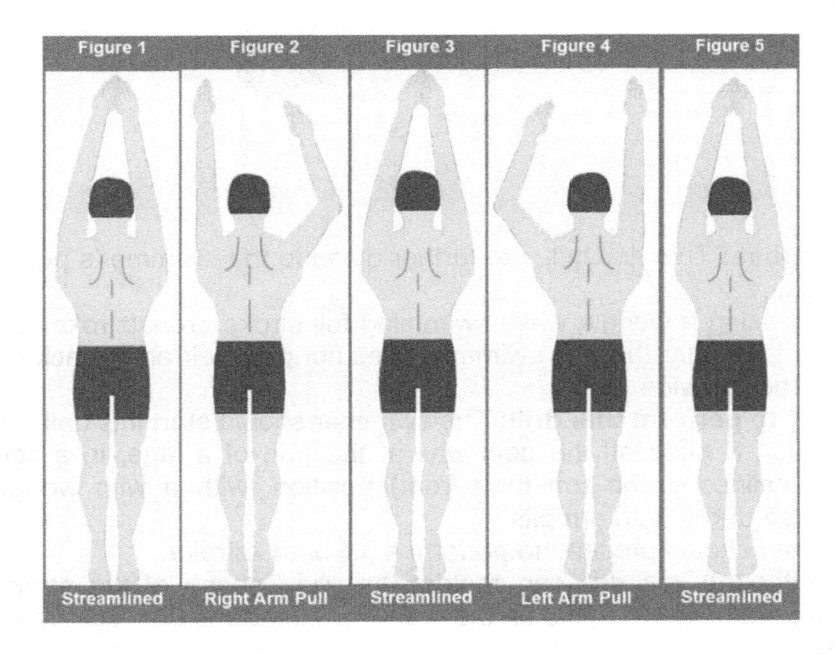

Purpose: This drill helps to further develop the swimmer's pulling skills.

How to perform this drill: The swimmer should start this drill with a push & glide off the pool wall at the end of a lane, in a tight streamlined prone (on their front) position.

- They should fully extend both arms above their head in a streamlined position (figure 1).
- Then they perform a single arm pull with their right arm (figure 2).
- The swimmer should ensure that their right arm finishes the stroke back into a fully extended streamlined position (figure 3).
- Once the swimmer's right arm has 'caught up' with and is alongside their fully extended left arm (figure 4).
- The swimmer should ensure that their left arm finishes the stroke back into a fully extended streamlined position (figure 5).

- They should repeat this drill for one length/lap of the pool (25m).

5.3: Pull with a woggle

Purpose: This drill helps to further develop the swimmer's pulling skills.

- By using a woggle while swimming full stroke breaststroke, can help to ensure that the swimmer does not pull their arms back too far and too wide.

How to perform this drill: The swimmer should start this drill with a push & glide off the pool wall at the end of a lane, in a tight streamlined prone (on their front) position, with a with woggle tucked under both armpits.

- They should proceed to perform a full breaststroke.
- Although this drill can restrict the glide phase of the stroke, swimmers should focus on the timing of their arms and legs, to aid propulsion.
- The swimmer should repeat this drill for one length/lap of the pool (25m).

Pull buoy pulling drills

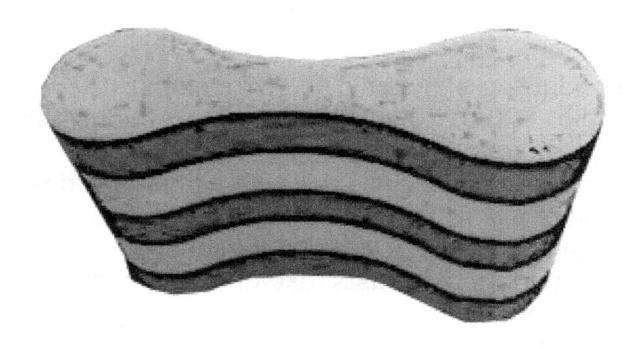

Introduction: The use of a pull buoy is an excellent way of isolating the swimmer's arms to develop their technique and to maintain their upper body strength.

● A pull buoy is an essential part of any competitive swimmer's kit. Although a pull buoy can be restrictive, the swimmer should focus on maintaining a smooth and long stroke.

5.4: Pull with a pull buoy

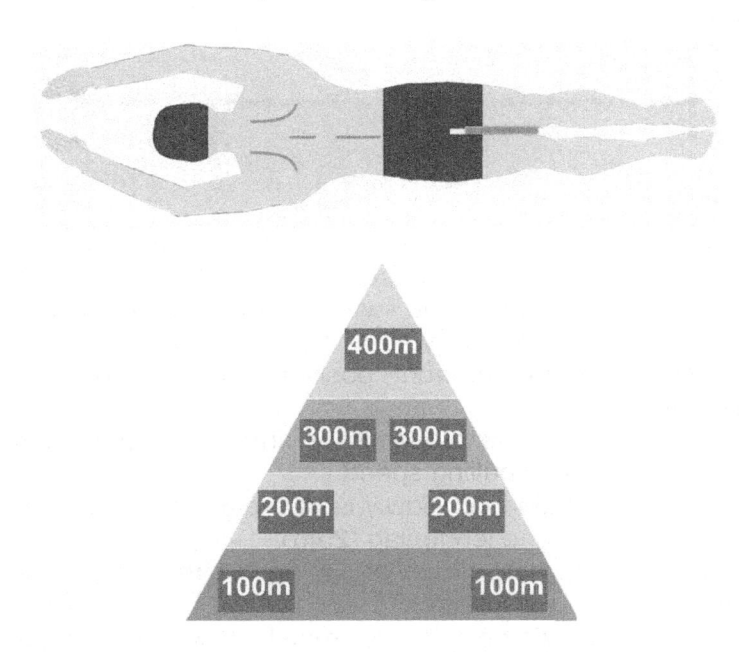

Purpose: This is a classic arm pulling drill, which is a great way of developing and maintaining an effective arm stroke.

How to perform this drill: This drill can be conducted over repeat sets of 100m/200m.

- I prefer, conducting a 'pyramid' in 100m steps.
- For example, 100m, 200m, 300m, 400m, 300m, 200m, 100m (steps of 50m for younger swimmers).
- The swimmer should start this drill with a push & glide off the pool wall at the end of a lane, in a tight streamlined prone (on their front) position, with a pull buoy between their thighs.
- They should perform a breaststroke arm stroke only.
- They should ensure that during the recovery they keep their elbows tucked in close to their body to prevent unnecessary drag.
- The swimmer should ensure that there is a distinctive glide phase at the end of each stroke.
- Their feet should be in a pointed (plantar flexion) position throughout this drill.

5.5: Pull with a pull buoy - builds

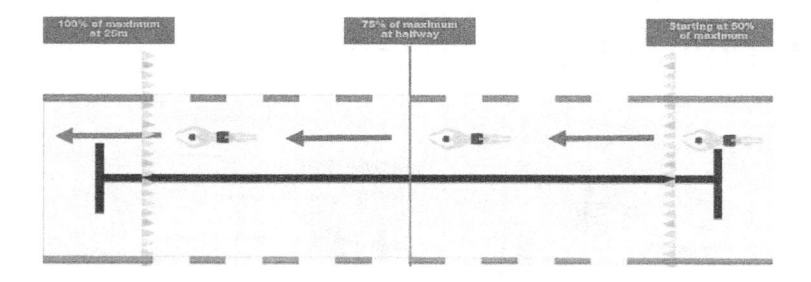

Purpose: This is an introductory speed play drill which helps strengthen and develop the breaststroke arm pull.

How to perform this drill: The swimmer should start this drill with a push & glide off the pool wall at the end of a lane, in a tight streamlined prone (on their front) position, with a pull buoy placed between their thighs.

- They should perform a breaststroke arm pull at approximately 50% of their maximum pulling speed.
- The swimmer should then slowly increase the speed of their pull over the distance of one length/lap (25m).
- They should pull with a high elbow on the recovery phase, to assist maximum stroke length
- The swimmer should be at approximately 75% of their maximum pulling speed at halfway and be close to reaching their maximum arm speed as they approach the finish of the length/lap.

5.6: Pull with streamlined legs

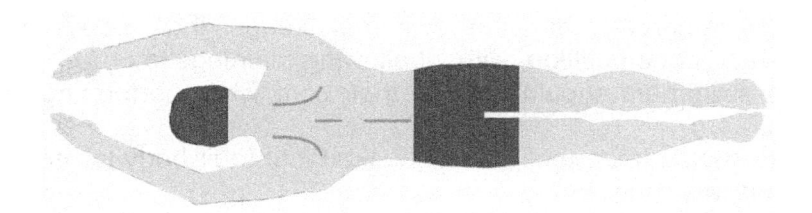

Purpose: This is an arm pulling drill, without a pull buoy which combines arm pulling and core strength development.

How to perform this drill: For this drill, the swimmer removes their pull buoy but still performs a breaststroke arm stroke only, while keeping their legs in a motionless, streamlined position.

● It is important that the swimmer keeps their body in a horizontal/prone position, without allowing their legs to drop.

● The swimmer should start this drill with a push & glide off the pool wall at the end of a lane, in a tight streamlined prone (on their front) position.

● They should engage their core while performing this drill*.

● The swimmer should keep their elbows tucked into their body to prevent unnecessary drag.

● They should ensure that there is a distinctive glide phase at the end of each stroke

● The swimmer should repeat this drill for one length/lap of the pool (25m).

5.7: Pull with crossed legs

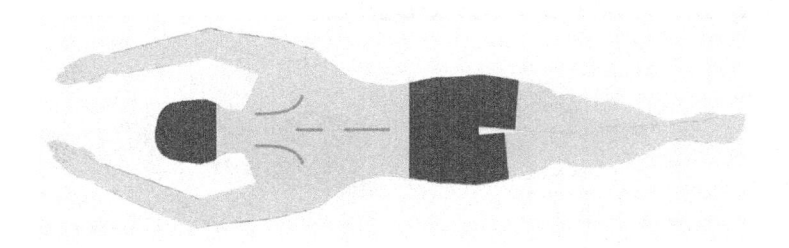

Purpose: This is a further arm pulling drill, without a pull buoy which combines arm pulling and core strength development.

How to perform this drill: The swimmer should start this drill with a push & glide off the pool wall at the end of a lane, in a tight

streamlined prone (on their front) position.
- They proceed to perform a breaststroke arm stroke only while keeping their legs crossed.
- It is important that the swimmer keeps their body in a horizontal/prone position, without allowing their legs to drop.
- The swimmers should engage their core while performing this drill*.
- They should keep their elbows tucked into their body to prevent unnecessary drag.
- They should ensure that there is a distinctive glide phase at the end of each stroke
- The swimmer should repeat this drill for one length/lap of the pool (25m).

*How to engage your core

Engaging your core muscles ensures they are correctly aligned, to help support and perform certain swimming drills and skills effectively.
- To engage their core, swimmers should continue to breathe normally.
- They should then tighten/contract their stomach muscles while drawing their navel towards their spine.

Core strength development

To effectively engage their core whilst swimmers should develop their core strength.
- Swimmers should perform core development training exercises such as crunches and planks as a regular part of their dryland/ land training programme.

5.8: Pull with a kickboard

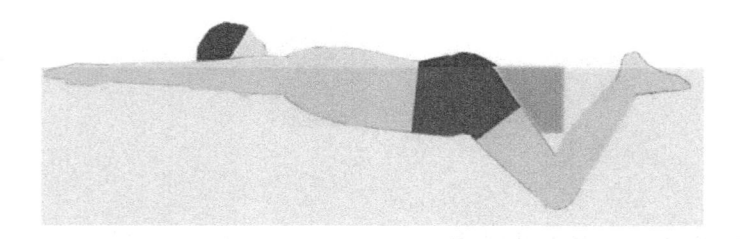

Purpose: This drill uses a kickboard to add extra resistance and help develop a swimmer's breaststroke arm speed and power.
How to perform this drill: The swimmer should start this drill with

a push & glide off the pool wall at the end of a lane, in a tight streamlined prone (on their front) position.
- Their legs should be bent at an approximate ninety-degrees angle and have a kickboard between their thighs.
- They proceed to perform a breaststroke arm stroke only.
- The swimmer should perform this drill with a quick and narrow arm pull
- They should allow a short one-second glide at the end of the pull.
- The swimmer should repeat this drill for one length/lap of the pool (25m).

5.9: Pull with pull buoy & hand paddles

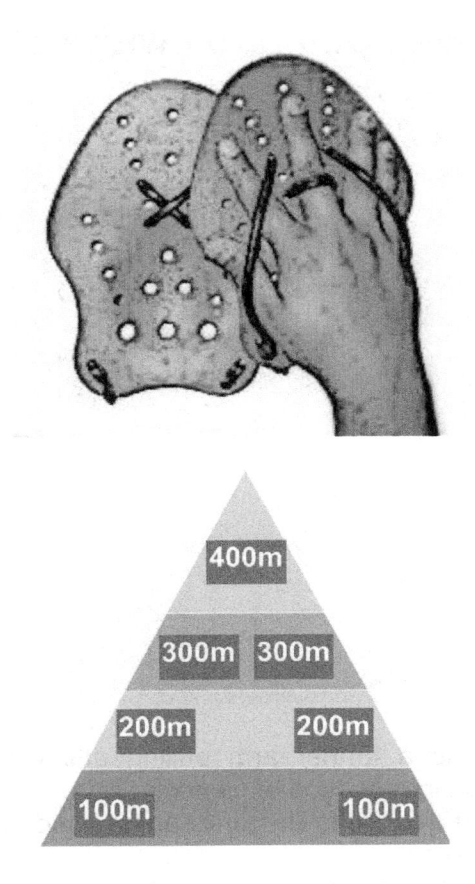

Purpose: This is a further arm pulling drill which adds extra resistance, is by the introduction of hand paddles, and in doing so this helps further strengthen and develop the breaststroke arm pull.

- They come in many different varieties, please ensure your swimmers have the correct type of hand paddles for their size and ability.

How to perform this drill: This drill can be conducted over repeat sets of 100m/200m.

- I prefer conducting a 'pyramid' in 100m steps.
- For example, 100m, 200m, 300m, 400m, 300m, 200m, 100m (steps of 50m for younger swimmers).
- The swimmer should pull with a high elbow on the recovery phase, to assist maximum stroke length.
- They should ensure that there is a distinctive glide phase at the end of each stroke.

5.10: Pull with pull buoy with fists

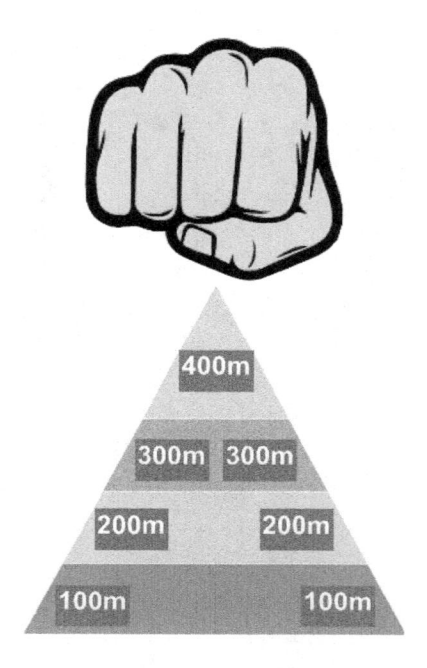

Purpose: This is a further arm pulling drill which adds extra resistance by the introduction of clenched fists.

How to perform this drill: This drill can be conducted over repeat sets of 100m/200m.

- I prefer conducting a 'pyramid' in 100m steps.
- For example, 100m, 200m, 300m, 400m, 300m, 200m, 100m (steps of 50m for younger swimmers).
- For this drill as well as a pull buoy, swimmers pull while clenching

their fists.

- This adds extra resistance to the arm pull and necessitates the swimmer pulling longer and harder and using their forearms as means of propulsion.
- The swimmer should ensure that during the recovery that they keep their elbows tucked into the body to prevent unnecessary drag.
- They should ensure that there is a distinctive glide phase at the end of each stroke
- Often once swimmers have completed this drill with fists when they go back to normal pulling with unclenched fists, most swimmers develop a better feel for the water and therefore some swimmers pull more effectively.
- They should ensure that there is a distinctive glide phase at the end of each stroke.

5.11: Pull with fists and open hands

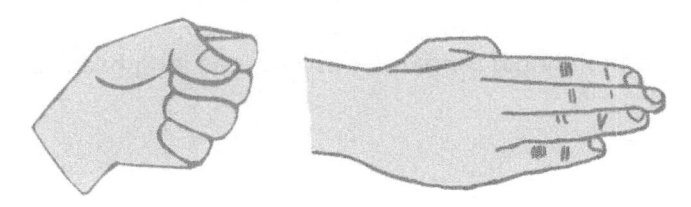

Purpose: This is a further arm pulling drill which can develop the swimmer's 'feel for the water' by the introduction of an alternate clenched fist and open hand swimming.

How to perform this drill: The swimmer should start this drill with a push & glide off the pool wall at the end of a lane, in a tight streamlined prone (on their front) position.

- They should proceed to perform six full breaststroke strokes with clenched fists and then six full breaststroke strokes with a normal open hand.
- The swimmer should ensure they have a high elbow on the recovery phase, to assist maximum stroke length.
- The swimmer should repeat this drill for one length/lap of the pool (25m).

Variations: This drill can be performed with or without a pull buoy.

- Once mastered the swimmer can perform this drill with alternate fists and open hand stokes.

5.12: Pull with tennis balls

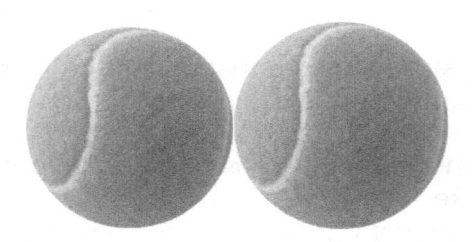

Purpose: This is a further arm pulling drill which adds extra resistance by the introduction of swimming with tennis balls.

How to perform this drill: The swimmer should start this drill with a push & glide off the pool wall at the end of a lane, in a tight streamlined prone (on their front) position.

• They should proceed to perform a full breaststroke stroke while holding a tennis ball in each hand.

• This drill can be performed with or without a pull buoy.

• The extra buoyancy generated by the tennis balls, requires the swimmer to focus on an effective pulling action.

• The swimmer should repeat this drill for one length/lap of the pool (25m).

Chapter 6: Breaststroke Timing

An effective breaststroke requires the coordination and timing of the three main phases of the stroke. Namely **the pull, the kick and the glide**.
● Even the most experienced breaststroke swimmers occasionally have difficulty with the timing of their stroke.

6.1: Pull Kick Glide 1-2-3

Purpose: This is an excellent introductory drill to help develop and maintain the swimmer's breaststroke timing.
How to perform this drill: The swimmer should start this drill with a push & glide off the pool wall at the end of a lane, in a tight streamlined prone (on their front) position.
● Swimming at drill pace (slow), the swimmer should perform a breaststroke pull following by a breaststroke kick.
● At the end of the kick phase, the swimmer should resume the tight streamline position and hold for three seconds.
● While doing so, they should self-talk "pull, kick, glide 1-2-3"
● This will help to help the timing of the stroke and ensure that the glide phase is effective.
● Swimmers should ensure they do not rush the count and maintain a tight streamlined position at the end of each stroke.
● The swimmer should repeat this drill for one length/lap of the pool

(25m).

6.2: Pull Kick Glide 1-2

Purpose: This drill helps to further develop the swimmer's breaststroke timing, by increasing the tempo.

How to perform this drill: The swimmer should start this drill with a push & glide off the pool wall at the end of a lane, in a tight streamlined prone (on their front) position.

● At the end of the kick phase, the swimmer should resume the tight streamline position and hold for two seconds.

● While doing so, they should self-talk "pull, kick, glide 1-2"

● Swimmers should still ensure they do not rush the count and maintain a tight streamlined position at the end of each stroke.

● The swimmer should repeat this drill for one length/lap of the pool (25m).

6.3: Breaststroke speed drill

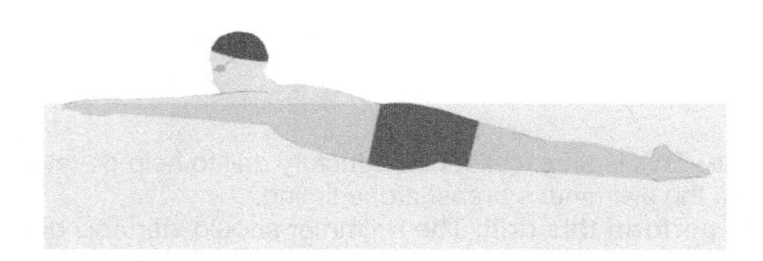

Purpose: This is an excellent drill for developing the swimmer's breaststroke tempo.

How to perform this drill: The swimmer should start this drill with a push & glide off the pool wall at the end of a lane, in a tight streamlined prone (on their front) position.

● They should commence with this drill by performing a hybrid stroke of breaststroke arms with butterfly legs.

● They should ensure that their head is above the surface at all times.

● The swimmer should perform quick, small and narrow breaststroke arm pulls.

- They should ensure that their butterfly leg kick is fast and shallow.
- As the name of this drill suggests, this drill should be conducted at speed.
- Due to the intensity required for the drill, it should only be conducted over short distances (25m Maximum) and include a long rest interval.

Variation: This drill can also be performed with the swimmer wearing swim fins.
- Swim fins should greatly add to the speed of the drill and should, therefore, further quicken the swimmer's stroke rate.
- This drill can be especially useful for younger or inexperienced swimmers.

6.4: Breaststroke with an alternate leg kick

Purpose: This drill helps to further develop the swimmer's breaststroke tempo.

How to perform this drill: The swimmer should start this drill with a push & glide off the pool wall at the end of a lane, in a tight streamlined prone (on their front) position.
- The swimmer should commence with this drill by performing a hybrid stroke of breaststroke arms with alternate breaststroke and butterfly legs.
- They should ensure that their head is above the surface while performing the butterfly leg kicks.
- The swimmer should perform this drill for initially one length/lap of the pool (25m).
- The swimmer should perform this drill while focusing on keeping the stroke long and smooth.
- The swimmer should repeat this drill for one length/lap of the pool (25m).

6.5: Breaststroke with leg kick variations

Purpose: This drill helps to further develop the swimmer's breaststroke tempo.

How to perform this drill: The swimmer should start this drill with a push & glide off the pool wall at the end of a lane, in a tight streamlined prone (on their front) position.

• The swimmer should conduct this drill by performing a hybrid stroke of breaststroke arms with, three breaststroke leg kicks, three butterfly leg kicks and three freestyle leg kicks.

• The swimmer should perform this drill for initially one length/lap of the pool (25m).

6.6: Combination drill

Purpose: This drill helps to further develop the swimmer's breaststroke tempo.

How to perform this drill: The swimmer should start this drill with a push & glide off the pool wall at the end of a lane, in a tight streamlined prone (on their front) position.

• The swimmer should conduct this drill by performing a combination of three streamlined kicks, three arms pulls with no leg kick, three speed drills and finally three full strokes at max speed.

• The swimmer should perform this drill for initially one length/lap of the pool (25m).

Variation: Once mastered the swimmer should reduce the number of strokes to two and perform of, two streamlined kicks, two arm pulls with no leg kick, two speed drills and finally two full strokes at max speed.

6.7: Shooters drill

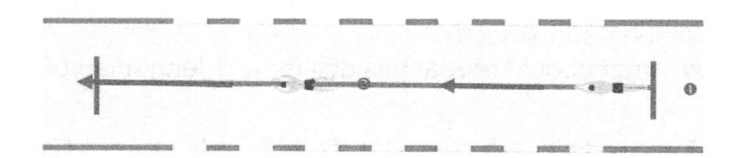

Purpose: This is an excellent drill for further developing both speed endurance and underwater dolphin kicking.

How to perform this drill: The swimmer should start this drill with a push & glide off the pool wall at the end of a lane, in a tight

streamlined prone (on their front) position, about half a metre under the surface,
● The swimmer should perform ten underwater dolphin kicks at maximum speed.
● The swimmer should then rise to the surface and sprints the remainder of the length/lap (25m)
● The underwater dolphin kicks should be performed as quickly as possible.
● The breakout should be shallow enough to allow a smooth transition into a sprint breaststroke stroke.

6.8: Head position drill

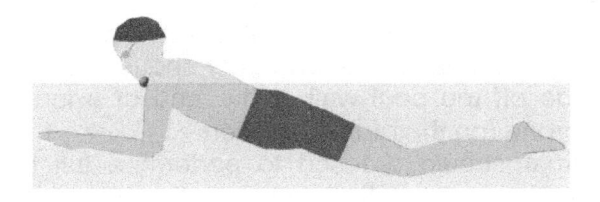

Purpose: This is a great drill for helping to stabilise a swimmer's head position while performing breaststroke.
● Some swimmers raise their head too far, which results in their hips dropping which causes extra drag.
● By using a squash ball can help to fix the swimmer's head in the correct position.
How to perform this drill: The swimmer should start this drill with a push & glide off the pool wall at the end of a lane, in a tight streamlined prone (on their front) position
● The swimmer should perform this drill by tucking a squash ball under their chin.
● They should look at the pool surface in front of them with their chin as close to the surface as possible, to help to ensure that their body position remains as flat as possible.
● Swimmers should complete this drill for one length/lap of the pool (25m).

6.9: 1 Arm 1 Leg Breaststroke

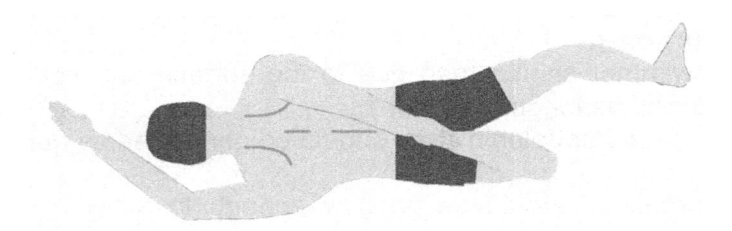

Purpose: This drill helps to further develop the swimmer's breaststroke tempo.

Please note: This drill is an advanced drill and should only be performed by those with the relevant flexibility.

How to perform this drill: The swimmer should start this drill with a push & glide off the pool wall at the end of a lane, in a tight streamlined prone (on their front) position.

- The swimmer should proceed to perform a full breaststroke stroke, but they grab one of their legs with their opposite arm.
- They should complete half a length/lap in this position and then revert to a full breaststroke stroke.
- They should ensure that they continue to swim with the same tempo as during the drill.
- Due to the intensity required for the drill, it should only be conducted over short distances (25m Maximum)

6.10: Swim builds

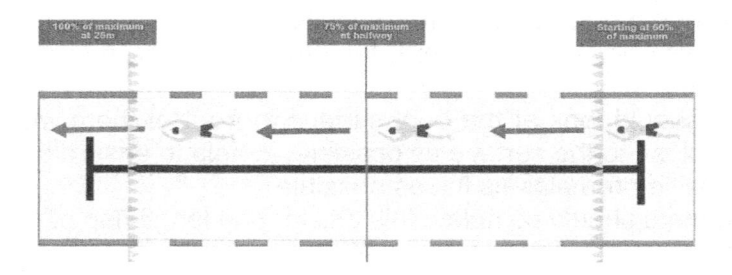

Purpose: This drill helps to introduce the swimmer to gradually increase their swimming speed.

How to perform this drill: The swimmer should start this drill from a push & glide from the wall at the end of the pool in a prone (face down) streamlined position.

- They should commence this drill by swimming one length/lap of the pool at approximately 50% of their maximum swim speed, with great technique.
- Swimmers should slowly increase the speed and should be approximately 75% of their maximum swim speed at half-way.
- They should be close to reaching their maximum swim speed as they approach the last turn flags and into the finish of the length/lap.

6.11: Easy/fast swims

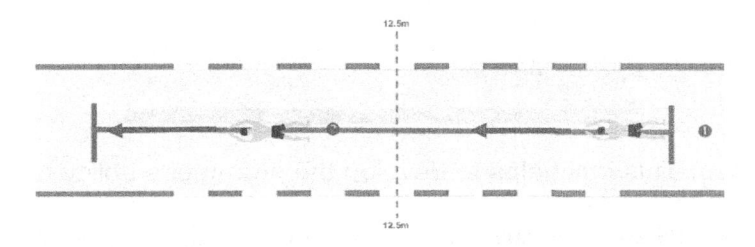

Purpose: This drill helps to further develop a swimmer's speed play technique.

How to perform this Drill: The swimmer should start this drill from a push & glide from the wall at the end of the pool in a prone (face down) streamlined position.

- They should commence this drill by swimming at a steady pace, with great technique for half a length/lap (figure 1).
- On reaching half-way, the swimmer should sprint for the remaining half of the length/lap, without the deterioration of technique (figure 2).
- A sinker or rubber brick on the bottom of the pool at halfway will aid this drill.
- For this set, swimmers will require one-part work to one-part rest.

Variation: This drill can be reversed so that the swimmer swims fast for half a length/lap and slow for the remaining half a length/lap.

6.12: Easy/fast swims

Purpose: This drill helps to develop the swimmer's ability to swim at varying speeds.

How to perform this drill: The swimmer should start this drill from a push & glide from the wall at the end of the pool in a prone (face down) streamlined position.

• They should proceed at a steady drill pace, with great technique for half a length.

• On reaching halfway, they should sprint for the remaining half of the length, without the deterioration of their technique.

• This drill can be reversed so that the swimmer sprints for half a length/lap and swims at drill pace for the remaining half a length.

• A sinker or a rubber brick on the bottom of the pool at halfway, would greatly assist the swimmer during this drill.

6.13: Easy/fast strokes

Purpose: This drill helps to further develop a swimmer's speed play technique.

How to perform this drill: The swimmer should start this drill from a push & glide from the wall at the end of the pool in a prone (face down) streamlined position.

- They should commence this drill by swimming with great technique for three strokes.
- The swimmer then performs three sprint strokes, again without the deterioration of technique.
- The swimmer should perform this drill for initially one length/lap of the pool (25m).
- For this set, swimmers may require one-part work to one-part rest.

Variations: This drill can be reversed so that the swimmer swims fast strokes then slow strokes.

- Once mastered, this drill can be adapted to increase the number of strokes i.e. five strokes easy/ five strokes fast.

6.14: Dead start - fast strokes

Purpose: This drill helps to develop a swimmer's speed and power

How to perform this drill: The swimmer should start this drill from a push & glide from the wall at the end of the pool in a prone (face down) streamlined position.

- They should commence this drill by performing a front-end scull.
- *For further information, see Chapter 4 Sculling: Front-end scull.*
- The swimmer continues to perform this scull for a count of ten seconds.
- The swimmer should then perform five quick full breaststroke strokes.
- The swimmer repeats this drill for one length/lap of the pool.
- This can be a very tough drill and should only be performed initially over distances of approximately 25m.

Chapter 7: Stroke Counting

Introduction: Stroke counting is a key swimming skill, which helps the swimmer develop and maintain a long, controlled, consistent and effective arm stroke.

• Stroke counting involves the swimmer counting the number of strokes (each time their hands enter the water) that they take to complete a given distance.

• Please note there is no one correct stroke count total, as swimmers are all shapes, sizes, abilities and strengths.

• Therefore, the number of strokes it takes to complete a certain distance can be different for each swimmer.

The key components for an effective stroke count are:

• A strong, quick and effective leg kick
• A strong, quick and powerful arm pull
• An effective glide phase aided by a great streamlining technique.
• Stroke timing ensuring the three phases of the stroke (the pull, the kick and the glide) combine for an efficient stroke.

7.1: Establishing stroke count

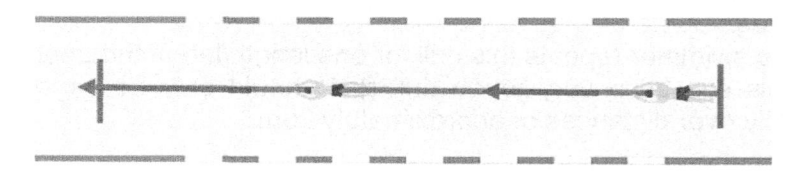

Purpose: This is the first in a series of stroke count drills, intending to establish a stroke count.

How to perform this drill: The swimmer should start this drill from a push & glide from the wall at the end of the pool in a prone (face down) streamlined position.

• They then proceed by performing full stroke breaststroke for one length/lap of the pool at a steady pace, with great technique.

• They should count the number of arm strokes they take to complete a length/lap.

• When they have finished this drill, it's important to ensure that they allow the swimmers swimming behind them enough room to allow them to complete the drill.

7.2: Reducing stroke count

Purpose: This is the second in the series of stroke count drills, intending to reduce their stroke count.

How to perform this drill: This drill aims to reduce the swimmer's stroke count by at least one stroke, per length/lap.

• The swimmer should start this drill from a push & glide from the wall at the end of the pool in a prone (face down) streamlined position.

• They then proceed by performing full stroke breaststroke for one length/lap of the pool at a steady pace, with great technique

• They may reduce their stroke count by stronger kicking, stronger arm pulls, better underwater kicking from the start, a better technical stroke or a combination of all of these.

• When they have finished this drill, it's important to ensure that they allow the swimmers swimming behind them enough room to allow them to complete the drill.

7.3: Holding stroke count

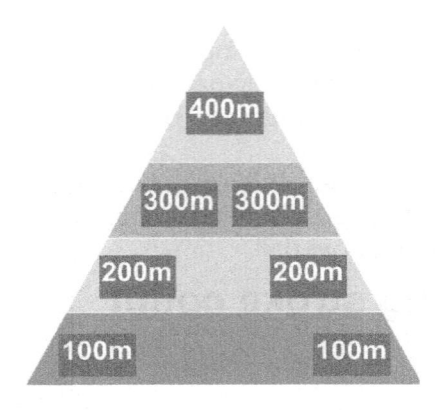

Purpose: This is the third in a series of stroke count drills, intending to hold their stroke count over a longer distance.

How to perform this drill: Once a regular stroke count has been established.

● The next stage is to 'hold' (maintain) a regular stroke count over a longer distance.

● These can be conducted over regular repeats of sets of 50m (25m for younger swimmers)

● The swimmer should start this drill from a push & glide from the wall at the end of the pool in a prone (face down) streamlined position.

● They then proceed by performing full stroke breaststroke for one length/lap of the pool at a steady pace, with great technique

● When they have finished this drill, it's important to ensure that they allow the swimmers swimming behind them enough room to allow them to complete the drill.

7.4: Stroke count with fists

Purpose: This is the fourth in a series of stroke count drills, intending to improve their stroke count by the introduction of swimming with fists.

How to perform this drill: The swimmer should start this drill from a push & glide from the wall at the end of the pool in a prone (face down) streamlined position.

• They then proceed by performing full stroke breaststroke for one length/lap of the pool at a steady pace, with great technique

• The swimmer should clench their fists and then go through the 'establishing' 'reducing' and 'holding' stroke count drills.

• Often once the swimmer has completed this drill with fists, when they go back to normal stroke counting, as a result, many develop a better feel for the water and therefore some reduce their stroke count.

• When they have finished this drill, it's important to ensure that they allow the swimmers swimming behind them enough room to allow them to complete the drill.

7.5: Stroke count min-max drill

4 x 50m	Rep 1			Rep 2			Rep 3			Rep 4		
	Stroke Count	Time	Total	Stroke Count	Time	Total	Stroke Count	Time	Total	Stroke Count	Time	Total
Swimmer 1	18	44	62	17	44	61	17	42	59	17	42	59
Swimmer 2	20	42	62	20	40	60	19	40	59	19	40	59
Swimmer 3	18	41	59	18	40	58	17	39	56	17	39	56
Swimmer 4	16	38	54	16	37	53	16	36	52	16	36	52

Purpose: This is the last in a series of stroke count drills.

• The objective of the min-max drill is to swim a given distance in the minimum amount of arm strokes with the maximum amount of speed.

How to perform this drill: For example, over 4 x 50m: A swimmer completes the first repetition in a time of 44 seconds with a stroke count of 18.

• By adding the number of seconds, it took to complete the rep, to the number of strokes it took to complete the set, this gives the swimmer a total 'stroke efficiency score' of 62.

• The swimmer's objective for the next repetition is to reduce their stroke efficiency score by either swimming faster, taking fewer strokes or a combination of both. (see table above)

• When they have finished this drill, it's important to ensure that they allow the swimmers swimming behind them enough room to allow them to complete the drill.

Chapter 8: Starts

Introduction: Many races, especially sprints, are lost even before the swimmers have entered the water, due to a poorly executed start.

● The development of a fast, explosive, racing dive with distance, should be a key objective of all competitive swimmers.

Key components for an effective start are:
The breaststroke start has three distinct phases: **off the block, the entry and the breakout.**

Phase 1: Off the block
This is the fastest part of the start, the explosive movement where the swimmer's feet leave the blocks.

● The swimmer should have a solid starting position, leaning forward on the balls of their feet.

● They should react quickly to the starting signal (gun, bleep etc)

● The swimmer should be explosive off the block, driving through their thighs, legs, balls of their feet and big toes.

● They should thrust their arms forward off the block, into a streamlined position, which needs to be maintained on entry into the water.

There are two types of competitive starts, **the track start** and **the grab start**.

Key components for an effective track start are:

- The swimmer places one foot in front of the other.
- Most swimmers put their stronger leg in the back position.
- The swimmer's feet should be approximately shoulder-width apart.
- The swimmer should be stable on the block and their weight should be distributed evenly between their front and back legs.
- The swimmer should curl their toes of their leading foot over the edge of the block, enabling them to push off the block with maximum force.
- The swimmer's head should be tucked down, with their chin resting on their chest.
- The swimmer should ensure that their hips as high as possible.
- The swimmer's centre of gravity should be positioned at the edge of the block.
- The swimmer's arms should be extended forward and grabbing hold of the front edge of the starting block with both hands, enabling them to pull themselves off the block with maximum force.

Key components for an effective grab start are:

- The swimmer should place their feet approximately 15cms (6 inches) apart.
- They should be in a stable position on the starting block by distributing the weight in their legs evenly.
- The swimmer should curl their toes over the edge of the block, enabling them to push off the block with maximum force.
- The swimmer's head should be tucked down, as close to their knees as possible.
- Their hips should be as high as possible.
- The swimmer should place their hands either inside or outside of their feet, whichever they find most comfortable.
- The swimmer's centre of gravity should be positioned towards the edge of the starting block.

Phase2: The entry
The entry into the water should be in a tight streamlined position, from which they perform the pull-out phases before the recovery.
- The depth of the dive should be deep enough to ensure that the swimmer can perform the three pull-out phases effectively.
- Namely **a butterfly kick, a breaststroke pull and a breaststroke kick underwater**.

Phase 3: The breakout

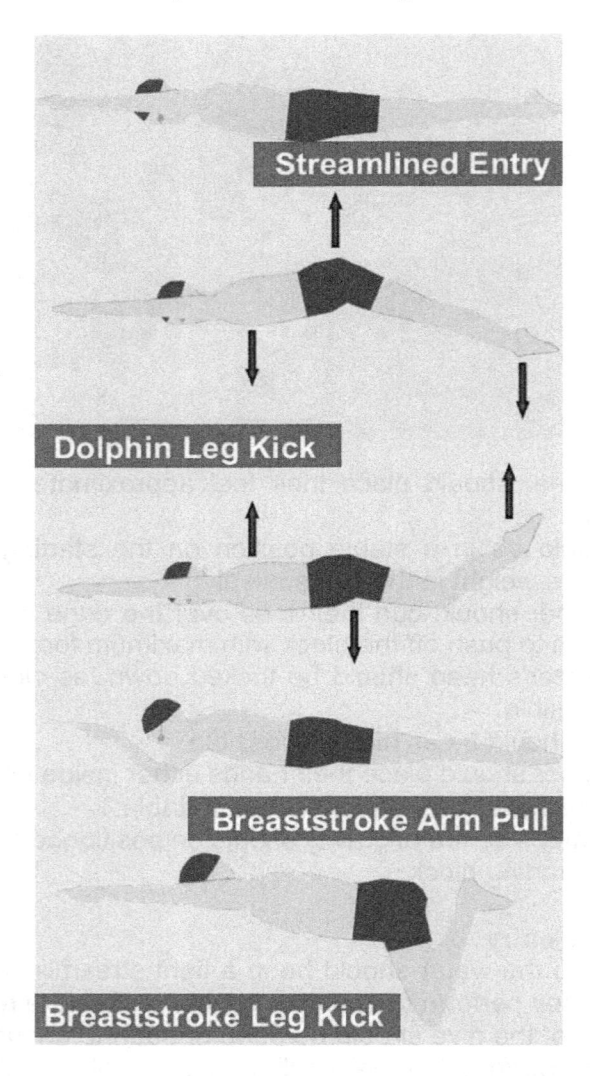

The series of movements to maintain speed and distance before the breakout into a full breaststroke.

- These are the **butterfly kick; the breaststroke pull and the breaststroke kick**.
- The swimmer should ensure that the speed initiated by the dive is maintained through each of the pull-out phases.
- There should only be the briefest of pauses between each breakout phase.
- The swimmer should ensure that each phase of the breakout is performed in a horizontal position.

- The butterfly kick should be fast and powerful.
- The breaststroke pull should be a powerful full stroke, starting from the streamlined position and finishing past the swimmer's hips.
- The swimmer should then shrug their shoulders and recover their arms close to their body, back into the streamlined position.
- The breaststroke kick should be performed simultaneously with the arm recovery.
- Some coaches prefer to teach performing the dolphin kick either during the glide phase or during the arm pull.
- However, many coaches believe that performing a dolphin kick after the breaststroke arm pull does not generate sufficient power and can even slow the swimmer's speed due to changes in their body position.
- As the swimmer performs the breaststroke kick in a streamlined position, they should naturally rise to the surface and be able to perform a smooth, quick and shallow break out into a full breaststroke stroke.

8.1: Poolside/Deck 'blast' jump

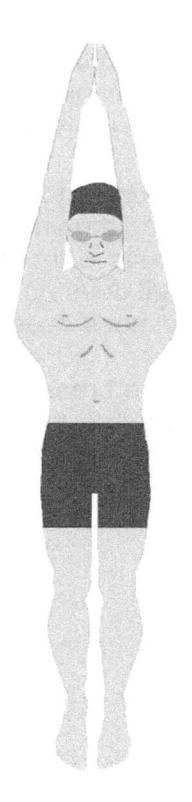

Purpose: This is an excellent poolside/deck introductory drill which demonstrates the explosive power required for a competitive start.

How to perform this drill: The swimmer should ensure that they find a safe space on the poolside/deck away from the pool's edge.

• The swimmer should start this drill, by squatting down on the balls of their feet, with their hands by their side touching the poolside/deck floor.

• On the command 'jump' the swimmer should perform an explosive jump upwards by extending their arms, legs and feet, into a tight streamlined position.

• They should ensure that they drive from the thighs, through their lower legs and finally from the balls of their feet through to their toes.

8.2: Finding the balancing point

Purpose: Often younger or inexperienced swimmers when starting to learn how to perform a competitive start, find it difficult to locate their ideal starting position on the block.

● This is the first in a series of drills to help find the swimmer's 'balancing point' on the starting block.

● The balancing point is the position where they are steady enough to ensure they are still before the starting signal, but balanced ready to blast quickly off the starting block to achieve a fast reaction time.

How to perform this drill: The swimmer should start this drill by assuming their preferred starting position on the starting block.

● In the swimmer's own time, they should roll forward on the balls of their feet, until they feel they cannot go forward any more without falling into the water but are in a stable starting position (their balancing point).

● They should then roll back to their original starting position.

8.3: Finding the balancing point with a dive

Purpose: This is the next in a series of drills to develop the swimmer's competitive start, by adding a dive to the 'balancing point' drill.

How to perform this drill: The swimmer should start this drill by assuming their preferred starting position on the starting block.

• They should then find their balancing point.

• They should then roll back on the block, then again, they should roll forward to find their balancing point.

• They should then perform a racing dive.

• They should ensure that they drive from the thighs, through their lower legs and finally from the balls of their feet through to their toes.

• They should also ensure that they thrust their arms forward off the block, into a streamlined position, which should be maintained on entry into the water.

8.4: Racing starts development

Purpose: The last in a series of drills to develop an effective competitive start.

How to perform this drill: The swimmer should start this drill by assuming their preferred starting position on the starting block.

- They should then find their balancing point.
- Then in their own time they should perform a racing dive off the blocks.
- To achieve a shallow racing dive, the swimmer should explode outwards off the racing blocks.
- If the swimmer dives too deep, it may be that the swimmer is not driving outwards off the starting block, but instead, they are driving downwards.
- If a swimmer looks down towards the bottom of the pool throughout the driving phases of their start, then this sometimes results in the dive being too deep.
- If the swimmer can lift their head for a split second, during the driving phase of their start, then this sometimes results in a shallower dive.
- Another common fault, resulting in a deep racing dive, is the swimmer's hands position.
- As the swimmer locks their hands into a streamlined position off the block, they should slightly raise the tips of their fingers, which raises their hands slightly, which may result in the dive being performed to the correct depth.
- The coach should give the swimmer feedback, regarding any technical adjustments that may be needed, and praise the good

aspects of their start.

8.5: Breaststroke underwater pull – introduction

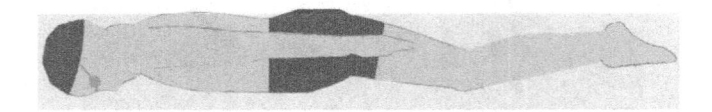

Purpose: This drill introduces the swimmer to the breaststroke underwater pull.

How to perform this drill: The swimmer should start this drill from a push & glide from the wall at the end of the pool in a prone (face down) streamlined position.

- The swimmer should hold this streamline position for approximately three seconds.
- The swimmer should then move their hands apart.
- They should bend their elbows while pointing their fingertip downward
- The swimmer should catch the water with both hands as they move their arms back towards their belly button.
- Their hands should finish the arm stoke resting on their thighs.
- The swimmer should hold this position for approximately two seconds.
- The swimmer should then return to the streamlined position by tucking in their elbows and moving their hands close to their body to reduce the amount of drag.
- The swimmer should then shrug their shoulders and recover their arms close to their body, back into the streamlined position.
- Whilst they are moving their hands back into the streamline position, they should perform a breaststroke kick.
- The swimmer should hold this streamline position for approximately one second.
- In which time the swimmer should be close to the surface
- The swimmer should then start their full breaststroke
- The first stroke should lift them to the surface

8.6: Breaststroke underwater pull – advanced

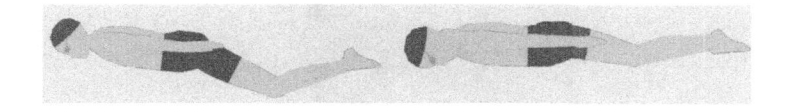

Purpose: To further develop the swimmer's breaststroke underwater pull, by the introduction of the underwater dolphin kick.
How to perform this drill: The swimmer should start this drill from a push & glide from the wall at the end of the pool in a prone (face down) streamlined position.

- The swimmer should hold this streamline position for approximately three seconds.
- The swimmer should then move their hands apart.
- They bend their elbows, while pointing their fingertip downward
- The swimmer should catch the water with both hands as they move their arms back towards their belly button.
- *Once the swimmer's hands are level with their head*
- *They should perform a quick and shallow underwater dolphin kick.*
- Their hands should finish the arm stoke resting on their thighs.
- The swimmer should hold this position for approximately two seconds.
- The swimmer should then return to the streamlined position by tucking in their elbows and moving their hands close to their body to reduce the amount of drag.
- Whilst they are moving their hands back into the streamline position, they should perform a breaststroke kick.
- The swimmer should hold this streamline position for approximately a second.
- In which time the swimmer should be close to the surface.
- The swimmer should then start their full breaststroke.
- The first full stroke should lift them to the surface.

8.5: Timed starts

Purpose: This drill helps to further develop an effective competitive start, by timing and recording the swimmer's start.

How to perform this drill: To test the effectiveness of a swimmer's start from the diving block.

● The coach should stand at the poolside/deck at 15m where a marker will be placed.

● The swimmer should perform a race paced start.

● As the swimmer passes the marker with their head, the coach should stop their stopwatch and record the result.

● The coach should give the swimmer feedback, regarding the time achieved, also any technical adjustments that may be needed and praise the good things about their start.

Chapter 9: Turns

Introduction: One of the key technical areas in swimming is the ability to perform a breaststroke turn efficiently.

● So much time, distance and energy can be saved by the execution of an effective turn, that turn drills should be a regular part of any training programme.

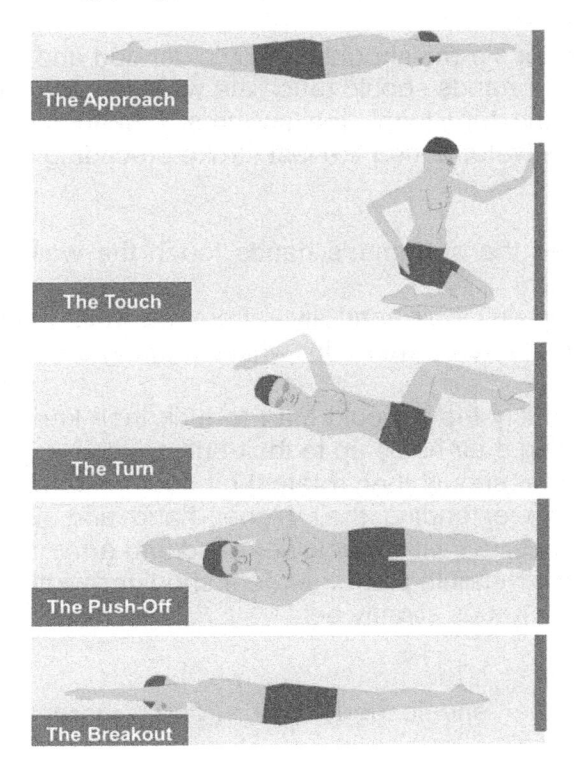

The Approach

The Touch

The Turn

The Push-Off

The Breakout

The key components for an effective open breaststroke turn are:

The approach
- A fast approach, the swimmer should maintain their race speed, going into the wall.
- This will help to ensure that they will transfer the speed generated going into the wall, through their turn and the push-off the wall.
- The swimmer should look at the wall 3 to 4 strokes from the end of the length/lap.
- With practice the swimmer should be able to adjust their distance into the wall.
- They should ensure that they kick into the wall, which will keep their hips in a raised position, this will help reduce drag and maintain their speed.
- The swimmer should not excessively glide into the wall, as this could result in a drop in their speed.
- The swimmer should ensure that they do not pull into the wall, which could lower their hips, thus increases drag and reduce their speed.
- The swimmer's arms should be fully extended and to make their turn legal, their hands should touch the wall simultaneously.
- To make the turn legal, the swimmer's head must break the surface of the water during the last stroke preceding the turn.

The Turn
- As soon as the swimmer's hands touch the wall, they should begin their turn.
- They should pull their hand away from the wall, on the side they prefer to turn, towards their hip, whilst keeping the other hand on the wall.
- Simultaneously they should start to tuck their knees up to their chest and bring their heels up to their butt.
- The swimmer should then rotate their body onto their side, while simultaneously extending their higher hand and arm to form a streamlined position with their lower hand and arm.
- The swimmer should plant their feet shoulder-width apart on the wall, with their knees slightly bent.

The push-off
- The swimmer should perform a strong, vigorous streamlined push-off the wall.

- They should aim for a depth of approximately 1m/3 feet, to help achieve the underwater movements and a smooth break out into their full stroke.

The pull-out
As with the start, the turn requires the swimmer to perform a series of movements to maintain speed and distance before the breakout into a full breaststroke.
- These are **the butterfly kick; the breaststroke pull and the breaststroke kick.**
- The swimmer should ensure that the speed initiated by the dive is maintained through each of the pull-out phases.
- There should only be the briefest of pauses between each pull-out phase.
- The swimmer should ensure that each phase of the pull-out is performed in a horizontal position.
- The butterfly kick should be fast and powerful.
- The breaststroke pull should be a powerful full stroke, starting from the streamlined position and finishing past the swimmer's hips.
- The swimmer should then shrug their shoulders and recover their arms close to their body, back into the streamlined position.
- The breaststroke kick should be performed simultaneously with the arm recovery.
- Some coaches prefer to teach performing the dolphin kick either during the glide phase or during the arm pull.
- However, many coaches believe that performing a dolphin kick after the breaststroke arm pull does not generate sufficient power and can even slow the swimmer's speed due to changes in their body position.
- As the swimmer performs the breaststroke kick in a streamlined position, they should naturally rise to the surface and be able to perform a smooth, quick and shallow break out into a full breaststroke stroke.

9.1: Push & glide in the prone position

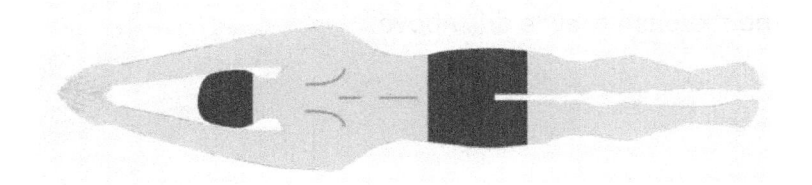

Purpose: This is an introductory drill to streamlining, an important skill in developing an effective turn.

How to perform this drill: The swimmer should start this drill from a push & glide from the wall at the end of the pool in a prone (face down) streamlined position, about a metre under the surface.

● They should attempt to get past the turn flags with their head (a good attempt) or their feet (a better attempt), before breaking out to the surface.

● The swimmer should ensure that they perform a strong push-off the wall.

● The coach should mark where the swimmer 'breakout' to the surface on the poolside.

● As a contrasting activity, ask your swimmer to perform a push and glide in the least streamlined position they can. This emphasises the importance of good streamlining.

9.2: Push & glide with underwater dolphin kicking

Purpose: A drill adding an underwater dolphin kick to streamlining, an important combination of skills in further developing an effective turn.

How to perform this drill: The swimmer should start this drill from a push & glide from the wall at the end of the pool in a prone (face down) streamlined position, about a metre under the surface.

● The swimmer should perform vigorous underwater dolphin kicking should as soon as they complete their push off the wall.

● This should result in the swimmer moving faster and further down the pool past the turn flags.

● The coach should again mark where the swimmer 'breakout' to the surface on the poolside and compare the difference between this and the push & glide drill above.

9.3: Push & glide with breakout

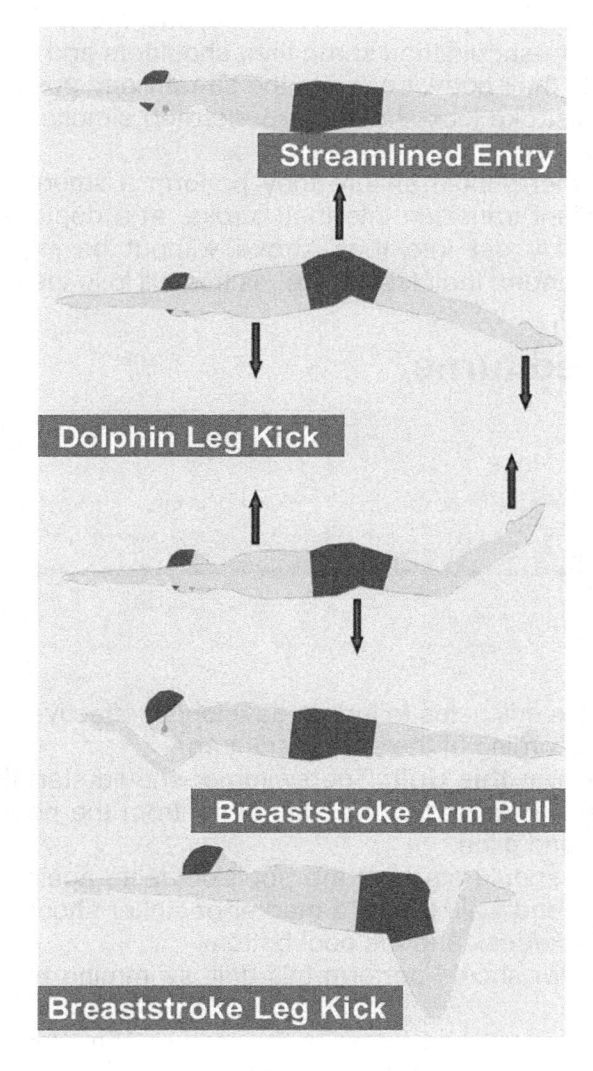

Purpose: A further drill to develop a fast turn off the pool wall.
How to perform this drill: The swimmer should start this drill from a push & glide from the wall at the end of the pool in a prone (face down) streamlined position, about a metre under the surface.
● The swimmer should then perform an underwater dolphin leg kick, a breaststroke arm pull and a breaststroke leg kick as they 'breakout' into their full breaststroke stroke.

- The underwater dolphin leg kick should be fast and powerful.
- The breaststroke pull should be a powerful full stroke, starting from the streamlined position and finishing past the swimmer's hips.
- The swimmer should then shrug their shoulders and recover their arms close to their body, back into the streamlined position.
- The breaststroke kick should be performed simultaneously with the arm recovery.
- The swimmer should ensure they perform a smooth breakout, with an efficient transition into their stroke, at a depth that allows them to quickly get into their stroke without having to stretch upwards to perform their first stroke, as this will lose the momentum out of the turn.

9.4: Timed turns

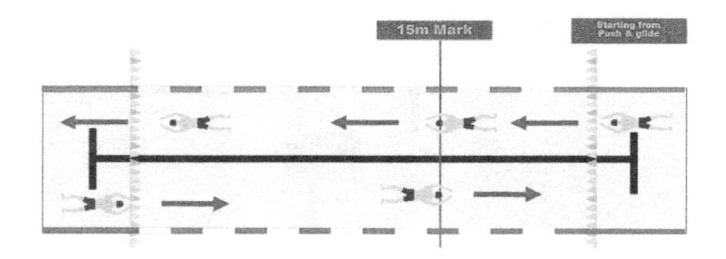

Purpose: This drill helps to further develop an effective turn, by the timing and recording of the swimmer's turn.

How to perform this drill: The swimmer should start this drill, in the water at the far end of the 25m away from the pool end wall, from a push and glide.

- The coach should stand at the poolside/deck, again 15m away from the turn end wall, where a marker or sinker should be placed on the poolside/deck and the pool bottom
- The swimmer should perform this drill, swimming at 100m race pace.
- As the swimmer's head passes the marker 15m from their turn, the coach should start their stopwatch
- Once the swimmer has performed their turn and has swum back past the 15m marker the coach should stop the stopwatch, record the result and feed the result back to the swimmer.

Chapter 10: Finishes

Introduction: Many medals are lost, and personal best times are not achieved, due to poor finishing.
● As for all key swimming skills, finishing needs to be a regular part of your training programme.

The key components for an effective race finish are:

● The breaststroke finish is the same as the approach and touch during a breaststroke turn.
● Maintenance of both speed and technique during the approach.
● A powerful two-handed simultaneous lunge onto the wall at the finish.
● The touch should be on a full powerful fully extended stroke, without an excess glide.

The approach

● It's important that the swimmer maintains both their speed and technique over their preferred finishing distance.
● The swimmer should 'spot' the wall from at approximately 5m from the finishing wall so that the touch is made on a full powerful fully extended stroke, without an excess glide.

The touch

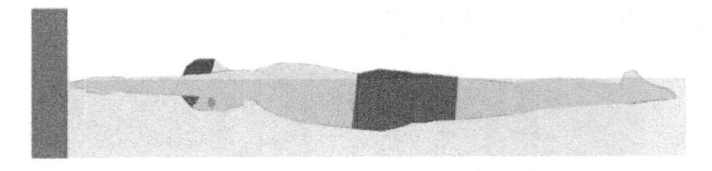

- The final stroke into the finish should be performed as a powerful simultaneous two-handed lunge onto the touchpad.
- The swimmer's elbows are allowed to be clear of the surface during the lunge to the wall.
- To ensure non-disqualification, the swimmer's hands should be separated when performing the touch.
- They cannot be overlapping, with one hand on top of the other.
- However, the hands do not need to be at the same height as each other.
- For example, one hand could be above the surface and the other hand could below the surface.
- During the touch, a swimmer may perform an addition arm stroke, without a kick.
- The swimmer can be completely submerged when they touch.
- However, if the swimmer is swimming with even-height shoulders the hands will likely touch the wall level at the finish.

10.1: Finishing from mid-pool

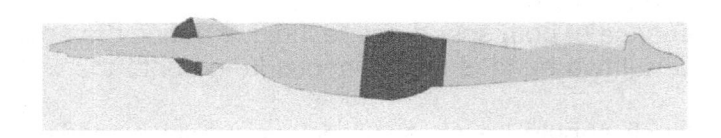

Purpose: This drill helps to develop an effective race finish.
How to perform this drill: The swimmer should use this drill to practice 'spotting' the wall to ensure they finish on a fast and powerful fully extended arm stroke, with a minimum glide.
- Starting in the water, 10m or 15m from the end of the pool, the swimmer sprints to the end of the pool and performs a powerful finish.
- They should begin this drill by lunging at the wall as the approach 'T', at the end of the black line at the bottom of the pool.
- During further attempts, they should make the necessary adjustments to ensure they finish on a fast and powerful fully extended arm stroke, with minimum glide
- Swimmers may wish the begin this drill swimming with even-

height shoulders.

● This can make it more likely that their hands will touch the wall level at the finish.

10.2: Timed finishes

Purpose: This drill helps to further develop the swimmer's finish, by introducing them to finishing on the pool wall.

How to perform this drill: Starting in the water, 15m from the end of the pool, the swimmer sprints to the end of the pool and performs a racing finish.

● The coach should stand at the poolside/deck, again 15m away from the turn end wall, where a marker or sinker should be placed on the poolside/deck and the pool bottom.

● The swimmer should perform this drill, swimming at 100m race pace.

● As the swimmer's head passes the marker 15m from their turn, the coach should start their stopwatch

● The final stroke into the finish should be performed as a powerful simultaneous two-handed lunge onto the touchpad.

● The swimmer's elbows are allowed to be clear of the surface during the lunge to the wall.

● During the touch, a swimmer may perform an addition arm stroke, without a kick.

● Once the swimmer has performed their finish the coach should stop the stopwatch, record the result, and feed the result back to the swimmer.

Chapter 11: Warm-Up, Cool-down and Recovery Swims

Introduction: The importance of effective warm-ups, cool-downs and recovery is well documented, although it is still an area often overlooked in many training programmes.

• An effective warm-up can provide a swimmer with many benefits. These include,

• Increasing the swimmer's muscle temperature, which can help reduce the chances of muscle or tendon injuries.

• It can help increase the flexibility of the muscles, helping them become more efficient and powerful.

• It can help prepare the swimmer's nervous system, making them more efficient and quicker to react.

• An effective warm-up can help to ensure that the swimmer's cardiovascular system is prepared for the body's increased demands for blood and oxygen.

• During training there is a need to actively recover to ensure the swimmer is not overly fatigued as to impair the swimmer's technique.

• After training and competition, the swimmer should perform an effective cool-down to aid muscle repair and help their recovery between training sessions or competition.

• It's, therefore, important to the swimmer's performance, to develop individual warm-up and cool-down protocols, which can be tailored to the individual swimmer and adapted to most training or competitive situations.

Examples of training and competition warm-up and cool-down protocols:

Warm-up 1: Dryland warm-up (blood flow stretching):
● Usually conducted on the poolside/deck before entering the water.
● This is to help ensure that the swimmer's muscles have an adequate blood supply and are warm and supple before swimming.
Warm-up 2: The short pool warm-up:
● Sometimes swimmers only get a few minutes to warm-up in the pool.
● Therefore, it's important that the swimmer has developed an effective pre-planned short pool warm-up protocol.
● **Warm-up 3: The Championship pool warm-up:**
● When competing at a major event the swimmer usually gets up to an hour in the water to warm-up.
Warm-up 4: Pre-Race warm-up (blood flow stretching)
● A swimmer could have to wait for an hour or before their event.
● Therefore, it's important that the swimmers wake up their muscles and help increase the blood flowing through their body again.
● Ideally, this should be a 10-minute routine before the call up to their race.
Cool-down 1: Post competition swim down:
● After any intense swimming activity, the swimmer's body and their nervous systems should have time to repair and recover.
● Usually, the sooner the swimmer conducts their swim down the more effective the cool-down.
Cool-down 2: Post competition cool-down (blood flow stretching).
● Swim down facilities are not always available at every meet/gala.
● The swimmer should get into the habit of stretching, walking or skipping after their race, to help their body and nervous system repair and recover.

Key components for a warm-up, cool-down and recovery swims are:
● The swimmer should start with a slow, smooth controlled freestyle or backstroke swimming
● They should slowly introduce breaststroke.
● They should vary the tempo to include stroke counting, drills, speed play, timed short sprints or starts from blocks (15m)
● Swimmers should keep moving during their warm-up to ensure their muscles are properly warmed up and their blood starts to flow.

Breaststroker's knee
A common ailment amongst breaststrokers is a condition known as breaststroker's knee, due to the high demands placed on a swimmer's knees during the breaststroke.
● One of the best ways to prevent breaststroker's knee is to warm-up and cool-down correctly.

A breaststroker's warm-up should ideally consist of the following:
● 400m easy and controlled freestyle and/or backstroke swimming
● This can be followed by 200m of mixed breaststroke sculling and drills
● This can be followed by 200m of easy and control breaststroke (such as the American warm-up drill below)
● Finally finished off with 200m of speed play/tempo drills.

11.1: American warm-up drill – strokes

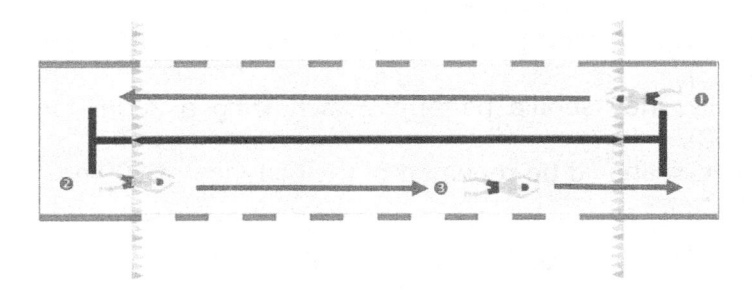

Purpose: This is an excellent warm-up drill, which requires the swimmer to perform a required number of strokes at a varying pace.
How to perform this drill: The swimmer should start this drill from a push & glide from the wall at the end of the pool in a prone (face down) streamlined position.
● The swimmer should proceed with this drill by performing eighteen strokes (each time the swimmer's hands enters the water) at drill pace, with their best technique (figure 1).
● They should then perform twelve strokes building to a 200m race pace (figure 2).
● Finally, they should perform six strokes holding a 200m race pace (figure3).
● This drill should be repeated of the distance of 200m has been completed.

11.2: American warm-up drill – distance

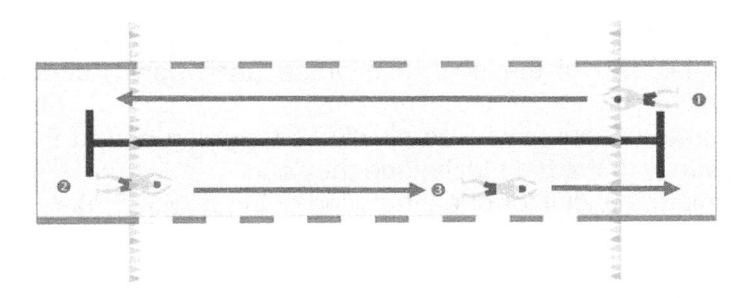

Purpose: This is an excellent warm-up drill, which requires the swimmer to swim certain distances at a varying pace.
How to perform this drill: The swimmer should start this drill from a push & glide from the wall at the end of the pool in a prone (face

down) streamlined position.
● The swimmer should proceed with this drill by performing 75m at drill pace, with their best technique (figure 1).
● They should then perform 50m building to a 200m race pace (figure 2).
● Finally, they should perform 25m holding a 200m race pace (figure 3).
● This drill should be repeated of the distance of 200m has been completed.

11.3: Super slow swimming

Purpose: This drill helps a swimmer focus on their stroke technique.
How to perform this drill: This is an excellent drill to improve all-round breaststroke technique, especially for younger swimmers.
●The swimmer should start this drill from a push & glide from the wall at the end of the pool in a prone (face down) streamlined position.
● Swimmers should swim as slowly as they can and at the same time swim with the best technique they can.
● Complete this drill for one length/lap of the pool (25m).

Chapter 12: Swimming Glossary

Introduction: Our swimming glossary contains a list of common competitive swimming terms with definitions, together with abbreviations and cross-references.

A

Aquatics: The collective (generic) name for any water-based competitive activity such as swimming, para-swimming, synchronised/artistic swimming, open water and water polo.

Aerobic Energy: The body's energy-producing system that requires oxygen.

Aerobic Training: The training system that requires oxygen. Usually involving long-distance swimming at a low intensity and a short rest interval.

Age Group Swimmers: Usually refers to swimmers under 16 years of age.

Anaerobic Energy: The body's energy-producing system that doesn't require oxygen.

Anaerobic Training: The training system that doesn't require oxygen. Usually involving short distance swimming at a high intensity and a long rest interval.

Anchor Leg: The final swimmer in a relay team.

Anchor Point: The point at the beginning of a stroke where the swimmer's hand/s starts to pull or push against the water at the beginning of the propulsive phase of the stroke.

Annual Training Plan: Usually formulated by the Head Coach during the closed season. This is an overall plan detailing the major objectives, championships and galas/meets for the up and coming season. It also outlines the different training periods for the season, together with an outline of what types of training activities will be performed.

Arm Stroke: The completion of an individual arm cycle, consisting of the pull phase, the exit phase and the recovery phase, before returning to the catch position at the start of the stroke.

Artistic Swimming see synchronised swimming

Ascending: Training set or rep on increasing times. Requiring a slower swim.

Assisted Training: Aided training that helps the swimmer to go faster than normal training or race speed i.e. swimming with fins or being pulled by a bungee cord.

B

B/C: An abbreviation for backstroke.

B/S: An abbreviation for breaststroke.

Back End Scull: A scull which focuses on the last part of the stroke before it enters the recovery phase.

Backstroke Turn Flags: Flags that are suspended across the width of the pool, 5m from the pool end to assist backstroke swimmers to gauge their turn.

Back-Up Time: The manual time which is given to a swimmer if they fail to stop the electronic timing system.

BC: An abbreviation for backstroke.

Beats Per Minute (BPM): The number of times that a swimmer's heartbeat for one minute.

Best Stroke: see main stroke

Bilateral Breathing: A breathing pattern requiring the swimmer to breathe on both sides of their body, while swimming freestyle.

BK: An abbreviation for backstroke

Blocks: see starting blocks

Boxes: The place at galas/meets where entry cards must be handed in before the start of the warm-up.

BPM: An abbreviation for beats per minute (heart rate)

BR: An abbreviation for breaststroke

Breakout: The transition from underwater to the surface, from either a dive or turn into the full stroke.

Breath Control: Sometimes called 'hypoxia training' which limits the number of breaths a swimmer takes.

Broken Swims: Training sets usually in two parts, an intense phase and a recovery phase. i.e. 4 x 150m as: 100m target times PB + 15 Seconds on 2.00, 50m O/C recovery on 1.00

BS: An abbreviation for breaststroke.

Builds: A training set, which requires the swimmer to start at a slow pace, and then gradually 'builds' speed into the swim.

C

Call Room see Whipping Area

Carbohydrates: The main source of energy found in foods such as pasta and potatoes, that should be a large part of a swimmer's diet.

Catch: The part of an arm stroke where the swimmer's hand enters the water and 'anchors' their hand in position before they start to pull or scull at the front-end of the stroke.

Chlorine: The chemical used in most swimming pools to kill germs and bacteria and help keep the water clean, clear and safe in which to swim.

Closing Date: The date when entries for a particular competition have to be received either by its organiser or the club's gala/meet secretary.

Club Championship: Premier internal club competition usually open to all members.

Conversion Times: Swimming times usually converted from short course to long course.

Core: The muscles in the swimmer's abdomen.

Cross Training: Any type of training outside of the water, that compliments a swimmer's training programme.

D

Deck: see poolside

Dehydration: The depletion of body fluids, usually caused by swimmers not drinking enough during training or competition. This is the most common cause of swimmers getting cramp and headaches.

Descending: Training set or rep on reducing times. Requiring a faster swim.

Development Gala/Meet: A gala/meet, to develop a swimmer's competition experience.

Did Not Compete (DNC): The initials used to indicate a swimmer who failed to compete in an event.

Did Not Finnish (DNF): The initials used to indicate a swimmer who failed to finish their event.

Did Not Start (DNS): The initial used to indicate a swimmer who did not start an event.

Disqualification Codes: These are codes used by gala/meet officials to indicate why and when an infringement of the rules has taken place, resulting in the swimmer's disqualification.

Disqualified (DQ): A swimmer is disqualified because, in the opinion of a poolside/deck official, they have infringed on the rules.

Distance per stroke: The amount of distance a swimmer covers during one complete stroke.

Diving Pit: A separate pool or part of a pool set off to the side of the competition pool. This pool has deeper water than a standard swimming pool, with diving boards/platforms. During a meet, this area may be designated as a swim-down pool.

DNC: see Did Not Compete

DNF: see Did Not Finish

DNS: see Did Not Start

Dolphin Kick: A kicking action used in butterfly, where the swimmer kicks with straight legs placed together.

Dorsiflexion: The foot position where it is flexed toward the front of the leg.

Down sweep: see sweep

DPS: An abbreviation for distance per stroke

DQ: see disqualified

Drafting: Swimming behind another swimmer, to save energy. This technique is used frequently in open water swimming.

Drag: The resistance caused by the swimmer's head, body or limbs, as they move through the water

Drill Pace: A slow, smooth and steady swimming pace, to enable the swimmer to recover and/or learn/concentrate on their technique.

Drill: A series of exercises and activities, used to develop a swimmer's stroke which focuses on a particular stroke and/or particular aspects of the stroke.

Dropped Time: When a swimmer goes faster than the previous performance they have 'dropped their time' or performed a personal best time.

Dryland Training: See land training

Dual Clubbing: Where a swimmer, usually due to educational commitments, swims for two clubs. One at or near their educational establishment and the second club is usually their original 'hometown' swimming club.

Dynamic Stretching: The type of stretching which requires the swimmer to stretch while performing a full range of 'swinging' motions.

E

Easy & Smooth: Performing a swimming activity using minimum effort and with a great technique.
Easy: Performing a swimming activity using minimum effort.
EBP: Event Best Performance see Event Best Time.
EBT An abbreviation for event best time.
Electronic Timing: A timing system which is operated electronically and linked to the touchpads in the water at the end of each lane.
Entry Cards A swimmer receives an entry card from a competition organiser for each event that they have successfully applied.
Entry Deadline: A date when entries must be handed into either the host club or the club's competition secretary.
Entry Fees: The amount a swimmer is charged to enter an event.
Entry Limit: Each gala/meet may have a limit on the number of swimmers they can accept.
Entry Time: The event entry time a swimmer provides when applying to enter a competition.
Even Split: When a swimmer swims at an even pace during training or competition.
Evens: Reps within a set with even numbers.
Event Best Time: The best time recorded at a particular event, normally at an annual championship or gala.
Exit Phase: The phase of the arm stroke, after the pull phase and before the recovery phase, where the swimmer's hand leaves the water.

F

F/S: An abbreviation for freestyle.
False Start: Occurs when a swimmer leaves the starting block or is moving on the block before the starter starts the race. The swimmer will be disqualified for making a false start.
False Start Rope: see recall rope
Fartlek: 'Speed Play' a series of training swims at a varying pace, slow, medium and fast etc.
Fat: A source of food energy that should be a small part of a swimmer's diet.
Faulty Start: Occurs when a swimmer/s leaves the starting block

due to an error of an official or failure of the starting equipment. Swimmer/s should not be disqualified in these instances.

FC: An abbreviation for freestyle (front crawl).

File: A group of swimmers, swimming in a line, either in the same lane or on the same side of the lane.

Flexion: Bending of a limb or joint.

Flip turn: see tumble turn

Flutter Kick: A kicking action used in both freestyle and backstroke, where the swimmer kicks alternately with a straight leg kick.

Fly: An abbreviation for butterfly.

Foot Flexion: There are two types of foot flexion: pointing your foot (plantar flexion) and flexing it upwards (dorsiflexion).

Form Stroke: A collective term for either backstroke, breaststroke or butterfly.

Front Crawl: Another name for freestyle.

Front-End: A scull or drill performed at or to simulate the first part of the stroke.

FS: An abbreviation for freestyle.

G

Gala: A swimming competition

Goals: Short, medium and long-range aims & objectives set by swimmers at the start of each season and agreed by the coaches.

Grab Start: A start where the swimmer places their feet in a parallel position on the blocks.

H

Hand Timing: Timing system operated manually, by the use of stopwatches.

HDW: see heat declared winner

Heart Rate Training: Training set where the swimmer is controlled by heart rate levels.

Heat Declared Winner (HDW) Commonly used in galas/open meets with a large entry list and schedule, where heats are arranged with swimmers seeded by their entry times. Once all the heats have been completed, the placings for each age group are calculated from the times recorded.

Heats: A race held at a competition, usually consisting of swimmers with similar submitted entry times.

High-Velocity Overload: A type of training requiring swimming at full speed without breathing, rest of the set distance swim easy

HR: An abbreviation of heart rate

HRT: An abbreviation of heart rate

HVO: An abbreviation of high-velocity overload

Hypertrophy: The increase in the size of organs (i.e. the heart) due to training.

Hypoxia Training see Breath Control

I

I.M. Order: The stroke order of an individual medley – butterfly, backstroke, breaststroke and freestyle.

I.M.: An abbreviation for Individual Medley.

In sweep: see Sweep

L

Lactic: The body while intensively training, will breakdown muscle sugar (glycogen) using a process that produces an acidic by-product waste called lactate. Muscles may start to burn or ache as lactate acid accumulates.

Ladder Swims: see pyramid swims

Land Training: Training conducted out of the water to gain additional benefits beyond those which can be achieved by training in the water alone. These include increased power, strength, endurance, speed, and coordination.

Lane Line: see lane rope

Lane Rope: The rope with floating markers that separate the individual swimming lanes.

Lap: see length.

Late Entries: Meet entries from a club or individual that are received by the meet host after the entry deadline.

Lateral Position: Body and/or head position on the side.

Length: A single length (lap) of a pool is 'there and back' usually 25m (short course) or 50m (long course)

Lesson Plan: The plan formulated by the coach as a guide to objectives of a swimming session. It details the sets and drills to be performed during a training session.

Logbook/Swimming Log: A journal/diary/log for keeping all the swimmers important swimming documentation in one place. Used for storing documentation such as goal setting sheets, recording training and competition performance evaluation sheets. This is an important monitoring system to aid a swimmer's development and should be kept by the swimmer and reviewed periodically by the coach.

Long Bungee: Two bungees joined lengthwise, one end attached to the web belt, the other to a secure fixing.

Long Course: Competitions held in a 50m pool

M

Macrocycle: A training period of some 15 to 24 weeks, usually with its particular training emphasis and objectives.

Main Set: The primary training set within a training session, focusing on the session's objectives.

Main Stroke: The swimmer's best stroke, sometimes referred to as their 'number 1' stroke.

Manual Time: The time for a swim recorded manually by a timekeeper using a stopwatch.

Marshalling Area: see Whipping Area

Masters Swimmers: Swimmers usually over 19 years old, who have dedicated training sessions and compete in dedicated competitions.

Maximum Distance per Stroke: A drill/drill, to develop a long, smooth stroke to develop a swimmer's stroke length.

MDPS: An abbreviation for Maximum Distance Per Stroke

Meet: see Gala

Mesocycle: A training period of some 1 to 6 weeks normally with its particular training emphasis and objectives.

Microcycle: A short training period with its particular training emphasis and objectives.

Midpoint: A scull or drill performed at the midpoint of the stroke.

Mini Goals: A series of small goals, usually breaking down a larger goal into 'bite-size' tasks.

Mins: An abbreviation for minutes.

Monitoring: Performed by coaches when either observing, recording or evaluating a swimmer's performance or technique in training and/or competition.

Monthly Training Plan: An outlined plan of the month's training activities and objectives.

N

National Qualifying Time: The qualifying time needed for entry to a national championship.

National Swimming Championships: The premium national

swimming championships.

Negative Split: Swimming faster for the second half of the set distance than the first half

No Time Recorded (NRT): The abbreviation recorded on a heat sheet to indicate that a swimmer's time was not officially recorded.

NQT: see national **qualifying time**

NTR: see no time recorded.

Number 1 Stroke: see main stroke

O

O/C: An abbreviation for own choice

Odds: Reps within a set with odd numbers.

Official Time: The swimmer's race time, usually recorded to one-hundredth of a second.

One Start Rule: Most competitions use the one start rule, which means that any swimmer responsible for a false start will be disqualified and not given a second chance to start.

Open Meet: Events that are 'open' to any qualified club or individual, although there may be a qualification standard/time.

Open Turn: A two-handed touch turn completed for breaststroke and butterfly

Open Water Swimming: Swimming that takes place outdoors either in the sea, rivers, lakes or docks etc.

OT: see official time

Outsweep: see sweep

Over the Top Start: To save time at some galas/meets for freestyle, breaststroke and butterfly races, the swimmers from the previous heat, may remain in the water until the next race starts.

Own Choice: A stroke or drill of the swimmer's choosing.

P

Pace Clock: A large free-standing or wall-mounted clock with a single hand used during training to give the swimmers a start time for a drill, sets and rest periods.

Para-Swimming: The specialist arm of swimming that caters for all those swimmers who have a disability and wish to train and compete.

PB: An abbreviation for personal best

Perceived Rate of Exertion (PRE): A subjective scale of effort assigned by the swimmer and/or coach, after training or competition.

Personal Best: The best time a swimmer has done so far in a particular stroke or event, either in training or competition.

Psychology: see sports psychology

Physiology: The scientific study of the functions in living systems and their parts.

Plantar Flexion: The foot position where the feet are in a pointed position, which reduces drag and places the feet in the optimum position for maximum propulsion.

Pool Floor Markings: The lines on the pool floor indicate the centre of a lane. The 'T' at the end of the black line indicates two metres from the end of the pool.

Poolside: The area around the swimming pool reserved for swimmers, officials, and coaches.

Progression: A series of drills which when combined, breaks down into a 'progressive' order to help complete a more complex task.

Prone Position: A horizontal face-down body position.

Propulsion: The force that moves swimmers through the water.

Protein: Found in lean meat, milk and cheese, they are one of the main building blocks of body tissue and can also serve as a prime fuel source.

Pull Phase: The propulsive phase of the stroke performed underwater.

Pulse Rate: A method to monitor heart rate.

Push & Glide: Performed in the water at the start of a drill or set. The swimmer 'pushes' off the pool wall with their feet, and glides in a streamlined position, to commence the exercise.

Pyramid: A training set where the workload/distance goes up then down.

Q

QT: see qualifying time

Qualifying Time (QT): Times are necessary to enter most open meets, and all county, regional/state and national competitions. Some competitions will have upper and lower limits on their entry qualifying times.

R

Race Pace: Training at the same pace as the swimmer would race.

Rate of Perceived Exertion: a simple but effective method of monitoring and evaluating the intensity of a swimmer's performance during training and competition.

Recall Rope: A rope suspended across the width of the racing pool that is lowered to the water surface to stop swimmers, in the event of a false start.

Recovery Phase (arm/s): The part of the arm stroke, executed out of the water after the pull and exit phases, where both the arm and hand are returning to the catch position.

Recovery Phase (legs): The part of the leg kick is breaststroke that brings the swimmer's heels up to their buttocks.

Recovery: A drill, rep or set where the swimmer undertakes a slow and easy activity to allow the swimmer to recover from training.

Regional/State Qualifying Time (RQT): The qualifying time needed for entry to the regional or state swimming championship.

Relays: A swimming event in which four swimmers participate as a relay team. Each swimmer swimming an equal distance of the race. There are two types of competitive relays: A Medley relay, where the first swimmer swims backstroke, the second swimmer swims breaststroke, the third swimmer swims butterfly and the last swimmer swims freestyle. The other type of relay is a freestyle relay, where all the swimmers swim freestyle.

Repetitions: A group of swims within a set.

Reps: An abbreviation for repetitions.

Resistance Training: A form of training with added resistance, to build either strength and/or stamina. i.e. using tethered bungee/stretch cords.

Rest Interval: The period of rest and recovery during training between a set or a rep

RI: An abbreviation for a rest interval.

Rotation: A movement of the body in a forward (tucked) position when performing a tumble turn, or sideways when performing full stroke freestyle of backstroke.

RPE: An abbreviation for Rate of Perceived Exertion

RQT: see regional qualifying time

S

S/C: see stroke count

S/L: see stroke length

S/R: see stroke rate

Scratch: To withdraw from an event after having declared an intention to participate.

Sculling: A swimming technique, focusing on the pitch and position of the swimmer's hands and forearms in the water, to achieve propulsion.

Secs: An abbreviation for seconds.

Set: see training set

Short Bungee: One bungee with one end attached to the web belt, the other to a secure fixing.

Short Course: Competitions held in a 25m pool

Sighting: An open water swimming navigation technique. Involving swimming with the head raised out of the water.

Signing In: Required at certain galas/meets where swimmers are required to 'sign in' against each event in which they are due to compete.

Signing Out: Required at certain galas/meets where swimmers are required to 'sign out' against each event they wish to withdraw from.

Sinker: A teaching device designed to sink to the bottom of the pool.

Skins: A swimming competition swam as an elimination event over several rounds.

Spearhead (Final): The lane order for spearheaded finals is decided from times in the heats or semi-finals. The fastest qualifier usually swims in lane 4, second fastest in lane 5, third in lane 3, fourth in lane 6, fifth in lane 2, sixth in lane 7, seventh in lane 1 and eighth in lane 8.

Speed Endurance: To perform at near maximum speed for a sustained period.

Speed Play: see fartlek

Speeding Ticket: Awarded to a swimmer who swims too fast in a time graded gala/meet and will not be awarded points or medals.

Split: A portion of an event shorter than the total distance that is timed. i.e. a swimmer's first 25m or 50m time is taken as the swimmer swims their 100m race.

Sports Medicine: The branch of medicine dedicated to sports healing, prevention and rehabilitation.

Sports Psychology: The scientific study of the human mind and its functions in sport

Sports Science: The branch of science dedicated to sports performance.

Sprint Training: Training sets performed at faster than race pace.

Sprint: A swim at maximum pace.

SQT: An abbreviation for state qualifying time see Regional/State Qualifying Time

Squad: A group of swimmers of roughly the same age and ability who train together.

Squadron: A freestyle relay of usually 10 or more swimmers in each team, arranged boy/girl in each age group, with the oldest swimmer going last.

Starting Block: The raised platform at the end of each lane of a competition pool, use for all competitive starts.

Starts: The start of a training set, gala/meet, either directly from the poolside/deck or in the case of backstroke an in the water start, usually with the aid of a starting block.

Static Stretching: The type of stretching which requires the swimmer to stretch while standing still. i.e. when touching their toes.

Step Test: A form of training 'test set' which helps monitor the swimmer's fitness.

Streamlined: The 'torpedo' position adopted by swimmers during a start and exiting a turn to reduce drag and achieve maximum speed and distance through the water.

Stretching see dynamic stretching and also static stretching

Stroke Count (S/C): Counting the number of strokes per length, to enhance stroke length and consistent swimming.

Stroke Length (S/L): The length in which a swimmer performs a single arm stroke.

Stroke Rate (S/R): The rate in which a swimmer performs several arm strokes within a given time.

Submitted Time: Times used to enter swimmers into galas/meets.

Supine Position: A horizontal face-up head, body and leg position.

Sweep: A phase of the propulsive elements in an arm stroke, leg kick or sculling action.

Swim-Down: see warm-down

Swimming Log see logbook

Swim-off: In a heat/finals type competition, a race after the scheduled event to break a tie.

Synchronised Swimming: A combination of swimming, dance and gymnastics, performed to music, competing either in solo or team events.

T

Taper: The resting process in training for swimming competition. As a major competition draws near, the swimmer will "taper" off the distances swum, to enable the swimmer to compete at their peak capability during the competition.

Target Time: The time given for a swimmer to complete a set or rep, which usually includes the rest interval.

Teaching Pool: A pool, usually shallow or with an adjustable depth, that is specifically used for teaching. Sometimes used as a competition cool-down pool.

Test Sets: Training sets where the results are recorded to monitor a variety of criteria including the swimmer's fitness and/or the effectiveness of the training programme.

Threshold Set: A high-intensity training set, to train the swimmer to raise their fitness 'threshold' at which they can tolerate larger amounts of lactic acid.

Time Graded Gala: A competition which has its particular qualifying times, which swimmers must achieve before they can enter the event.

Time Trial: An event or series of events where a swimmer attempts to achieve a required qualifying time.

Timekeeper Timekeepers record the time for competitors swimming in their lane.

Touchpad: The removable plate (at the end of the pool) that is connected to an electronic timing system.

Track Start: A start where the swimmer places their feet one in front of the other on the blocks.

Training Camp: A training environment, usually at a different venue (sometimes overseas) where swimmers can focus on developing both their technique and fitness.

Training Overload: A type of training which overloads the swimmer with a series of intense training sets. The aim is that the swimmer adapts to this type of training and becomes fitter and stronger as a result.

Training Plan: see lesson plan

Training Set: A block of work during training, usually containing several reps and focusing on one type of training activity.

Training Systems: There are two main training systems. Aerobic: A system that requires oxygen and Anaerobic: A system that doesn't require oxygen.

Training Zones: The different types of swimming training i.e. anaerobic, aerobic, sprint etc.

Transition Turns: The turns in an individual medley that transfers the swimmer from one stroke to another.

Transition: The underwater phase between a start and the stroke or between a turn and a stroke.

Transitions (Triathlon): The period of a race where the triathlete transfers from one discipline to another. Either from the swim to the bike or the bike to the run.

Triathlon: A competitive event which comprises of three continuous phases, a swim, a bike ride and a run. Distances for each phase can vary.

TT: see Time Trial

Tucked: The position a swimmer should adopt when performing a tumble turn. Chin on the chest, knees on stomach and heels on bottom.

Tumble Turn: The competitive freestyle or backstroke turn, sometimes referred to as the flip turn.

Turn Flags: see backstroke turn flags

U

U/W: An abbreviation for underwater

Underwater Dolphin Kick: Performed by the swimmer in a tight streamlined position, with a vigorous double legged kick from below the knees. Commonly used during starts and turns for all strokes.

Undulation: The wave-like motion with the body a swimmer performs while swimming butterfly.

Unilateral Breathing: Breathing to one side while swimming freestyle. This can lead to an imbalance in the stroke over time. (see bilateral breathing)

Upsweep: see sweep

V

VO2 Max: Distance training sets where swimmers are asked to swim as close to their maximum oxygen uptake will allow.

W

Warm-Down: A series of pool and poolside activities used by the swimmer after training or competition, essential for a swimmer's recovery and important for avoiding.

Warm-Down Pool: A separate pool for swimming down after a competition, which is usually a teaching pool or diving pit.

Warm-Up: A series of pool and poolside activities used by the swimmer before training or competition. Essential to warm-up the muscles and stimulate the blood flow.

Weekly Training Plan: Produced by the coach and is an outlined plan of the week's training session.

Weight Training: Traditionally performed by senior swimmers, using free weights, but is increasingly performed using pulleys and levers, swimmers perform a series of weight resistant exercises to increase strength and power during their land training programme.

Whipping Area: A room or area used during competition, on or near the poolside/deck, where the swimmers assemble before their event.

Y

Year Age: Age-determined events are categorised by the age of a swimmer on a specific date, usually either at year-end or the date of the competition.

Youth Swimmers: Swimmers usually aged 14 -17 years for girls and 15 – 18 for boys.

Made in the USA
Middletown, DE
27 July 2023

35824366R00056